American Voter Turnout

TRANSFORMING AMERICAN POLITICS

Lawrence C. Dodd, Series Editor

Dramatic changes in political institutions and behavior over the past three decades have underscored the dynamic nature of American politics, confronting political scientists with a new and pressing intellectual agenda. The pioneering work of early postwar scholars, while laying a firm empirical foundation for contemporary scholarship, failed to consider how American politics might change or recognize the forces that would make fundamental change inevitable. In reassessing the static interpretations fostered by these classic studies, political scientists are now examining the underlying dynamics that generate transformational change.

Transforming American Politics brings together texts and monographs that address four closely related aspects of change. A first concern is documenting and explaining recent changes in American politics—in institutions, processes, behavior, and policymaking. A second is reinterpreting classic studies and theories to provide a more accurate perspective on postwar politics. The series looks at historical change to identify recurring patterns of political transformation within and across the distinctive eras of American politics. Last and perhaps most important, the series presents new theories and interpretations that explain the dynamic processes at work and thus clarify the direction of contemporary politics. All of the books focus on the central theme of transformation in both the conduct of American politics and in the way we study and understand its many aspects.

Books in This Series

American Voter Turnout: An Institutional Perspective, David Hill

Revolving Gridlock, Second Edition, David W. Brady and Craig Volden

The Congressional Experience, Third Edition, David E. Price

Campaigns and Elections American Style, Second Edition, edited by James A. Thurber and Candice J. Nelson

The Parties Respond, Fourth Edition, edited by L. Sandy Maisel

Diverging Parties, Jeffrey M. Stonecash, Mark Brewer, and Mack Mariani

Votes, Money, and the Clinton Impeachment, Irwin Morris

Class and Party in American Politics, Jeffrey M. Stonecash

Congress and the Decline of Public Trust, edited by Joseph Cooper

Public Opinion in America, Second Edition, James A. Stimson

Still Seeing Red, John Kenneth White

Masters of the House, edited by Roger H. Davidson, Susan Webb Hammond, and Raymond W. Smock

Governing Partners, Russell L. Hanson

Governance and the Changing American States, David M. Hedge

The Collapse of the Democratic Presidential Majority, David G. Lawrence

The Divided Democrats, William G. Mayer

Extraordinary Politics, Charles C. Euchner

The Irony of Reform, G. Calvin Mackenzie

Broken Contract, Stephen C. Craig

Young Versus Old, Susan A. MacManus

The New American Politics, Bryan D. Jones

Bureaucratic Dynamics, B. Dan Wood and Richard W. Waterman

The Dynamics of American Politics, Lawrence C. Dodd and Calvin Jillson

The Politics of Interests, Mark P. Petracca

American Voter Turnout

AN INSTITUTIONAL PERSPECTIVE

David Hill

Valdosta State University

A Member of the Perseus Books Group

Westview Press books are available at special discounts for bulk
purchases in the United States by corporations, institutions, and
other organizations. For more information, please contact the
Special Markets Department at the Perseus Books Group,
11 Cambridge Center, Cambridge MA 02142, or call
(617) 252-5298 or (800) 255-1514, or e-mail
special.markets@perseusbooks.com.

Library of Congress Cataloging-in-Publication Data
Hill, David.
  American voter turnout : an institutional approach / David Hill.
     p. cm.
  Includes bibliographical references and index.
  ISBN-13: 978-0-8133-4328-0 (hc : alk. paper)
  ISBN-10: 0-8133-4328-3 (hc : alk. paper) 1. Voting—United States.
  2. Political participation—United States. 3. Elections—United States.
  I. Title.
  JK1967.H545 2006
  324.973—dc22
                                                        2005022689

06 07 08 / 10 9 8 7 6 5 4 3 2

Contents

1   Introduction   1

2   Explanations of Turnout   11

3   Restricting Access to the Ballot Box:
    The Impact of Registration Laws on Turnout   33

4   Placing the United States in Context:
    A Comparative Look at Electoral Systems   59

5   Winner-Take-All Elections, Part I:
    The Electoral College: Strategy, Mobilization, and Turnout   71

6   Winner-Take-All Elections, Part II:
    Competition, Spending, and Turnout in U. S.
    House Elections   93

7   The Separation of Powers: Divided Government,
    Responsiveness, Accountability, and Turnout   115

8   Conclusion: The Future of Electoral Reform in the
    United States   133

Appendix A   *149*

Appendix B   *151*

Appendix C   *155*

Acknowledgments   *157*

References   *159*

Index   *175 to Lisa and Emily*

1

Introduction

At approximately 2:00 P.M. on November 3, 2004, John Kerry conceded the 2004 presidential election to President George W. Bush, thus ending a close, often bitterly fought campaign. By all accounts 2004 should have been a high-turnout election. It took place in the context of a controversial war and a controversial issue (gay marriage) that had the potential to mobilize voters on both sides of the issue. Additionally, both Republican and Democratic parties, along with their allied interest groups, waged extensive and intense drives to register as many new voters as possible ("Into the Final Straight" 2004), and they spent more money than ever before on a presidential election (www.opensecrets.org).

A record number of voters cast ballots on Election Day (123,675,639), the highest turnout for a presidential election since 1972, with the exception of 1992. The turnout rate for all individuals of voting age (VAP) was 55.3 percent, a five percentage point increase over 2000. The turnout rate for all citizens, excluding individuals ineligible to vote due to citizenship status or incarceration (VEP), was 60 percent in 2004, an almost six percentage point increase over 2000.[1]

Nonetheless, the turnout rate was a disappointment when compared with those in nineteen other industrialized democracies, including Great Britain, France, Germany, Italy, and the Scandinavian nations. These democracies have had an average 72.6 percent turnout in their most recent elections, as contrasted with 60 percent for the United States in 2004.[2] Thus American voter turnout was nearly thirteen percentage

FIG 1.1   Mean Turnout in Established Democracies, 1960–2000

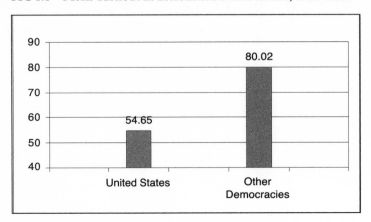

Source: International Institute for Electoral Assistance;
Federal Elections Commission

points lower, even in a highly competitive national election with a great deal at stake. Nor is the higher turnout in recent elections among the other democracies a recent aberration.

Figure 1.1 presents the mean turnout rates between 1960 and 2000 for twenty comparable industrialized democracies, including the United States.[3] The mean turnout rate for the United States between 1960 and 2000 was 54.65 percent, while in all other industrialized democracies the mean turnout rate over this time period was 80.02 percent. Figure 1.1 demonstrates clearly the substantial turnout difference between the United States and other industrialized democracies.[4] It highlights a crucial question about the nature of American democracy: Why is voter turnout in the United States so much lower than in other industrialized democracies, even in situations that seem primed to induce voter participation?

In this book, building on the extant research relating to national-level turnout, I argue that *the turnout in U.S. national elections is comparatively low mainly because the electoral, representational, and governmental institutional arrangements in the United States create an environment that constrains rather than facilitates electoral participation.* The core of the book will bring to undergraduate students and interested laypersons a systematic understanding of how American institutions have inhibited voter turnout when democratic institutions elsewhere seem more prone to facilitate it. My concern specifically is with why America lags behind other countries in voter turnout, not with the rise or decline in turnout across time among industrialized democracies. Since this issue can be confusing, I shall address it at the beginning of this book.

The Puzzle: Declining Turnout

In 1978 Richard Brody asked why turnout in U.S. elections had steadily declined since 1960, although factors that should facilitate turnout had increased, such as educational levels, and factors that constrain turnout, such as the exclusion of African Americans from the electoral process in the South, had been eliminated. This essay stimulated scholars to explain why American turnout was declining. In the 1960 presidential election, voter turnout was 62.77 percent. From that election forward, however, turnout steadily declined, reaching a low of 50.15 percent in 1988. Following the 55.20 percent turnout in 1992 (the highest since 1972), turnout fell to 49.08 percent in 1996, which was the lowest voter turnout rate since 1924.

In actuality, turnout decline has not been limited to the United States. Most industrialized democracies have experienced declines in the post–World War II era. Among twenty-two industrialized democracies, Franklin (2004) found that the mean turnout trend since 1945 was a 5.5 percentage point decline. Of the twenty-two countries, sixteen experienced declines in turnout since 1945, while only six experienced gains.[5] Rather than a symptom of democratic malaise in the United States, turnout decline appears to be a phenomenon occurring in most industrialized democracies (Franklin 2004).

Franklin (2004) provides a compelling explanation for national-level turnout declines (and increases) by arguing that if a cohort of young voters enters the electorate when elections are uncompetitive (i.e., they are low turnout elections), then turnout will decrease in future elections.[6] If a cohort (or cohorts) enters the electorate during a period of high competition (and thus high turnout), then turnout should increase in future elections. The logic behind this argument is straightforward. Given that voting is a learned habit, young voters coming of voting age during a low turnout period should continue to abstain throughout their lives and turnout should remain relatively low. If young voters come of age during a high turnout period, then they should continue to vote throughout their lives and turnout should remain high. Franklin's argument is based on two key factors. The first is that young individuals are socialized into modes of behavior. What happens to young people in their formative years impacts their attitudes and behaviors throughout their lives.

Franklin identifies the lowering of the voting age in many democracies to eighteen during the late 1960s and early 1970s as key to continuing turnout decline. He argues that these new eighteen-year-old potential voters were more susceptible to the electoral environment than their twenty-one-year-old counterparts. Each cohort of eighteen-year-olds that came into the electorate added a larger number of citizens with a low probability of voting.

The second factor (and strongly related to the first) is the "character of elections." Competitive elections, with strong, cohesive parties that present clear choices to voters, tend to have high turnout because citizen interest is heightened by the increased politicization of the environment. Franklin argues that at the same time countries were lowering the voting age, the character of elections changed in that the competitiveness of elections declined, and thus elections lost some of their mobilizing potential. Given that eighteen- to twenty-year-old potential voters are very susceptible to the electoral environment, their first experience in a low turnout election "socializes" them that elections are uncompetitive and uninteresting and consequently not very important. Each cohort of young people that comes into the electorate during a nonstimulating election period leaves a "footprint" in the electorate: as they age they remain nonvoters. Given the decline in competitive elections over the past couple of decades, many cohorts have entered the electorate in nonstimulating elections and thus turnout has continued to decline.

The other side of this argument is that if new cohorts of voters enter the electorate during a period of competitive elections, then these new cohorts leave a footprint of voters in the electorate and turnout should increase in future elections. National elections in the United States since 2000 have been very competitive and thus it is possible that the cohorts entering the electorate during this period will create a footprint of voting in the electorate and turnout will increase in future elections.

This argument appears to work well in the United States. The voting age was lowered to eighteen in 1971 by the Twenty-Sixth Amendment. This occurred as levels of competition in congressional elections declined (See Fiorina 1989; Mayhew 1974). Each cohort of eighteen- to twenty-year-olds that entered the electorate experienced low turnout elections, and thus a large proportion of each cohort refrained from voting. Across the 1970s and 1980s successive cohorts were socialized to not vote and turnout declined. Franklin also highlights the role played by the separation of powers system. Because policymaking power is fragmented between the executive and legislative branches, the government is less responsive to the demands of the electorate. Additionally the system reduces citizens' ability to assess governmental performance and accountability is therefore reduced. Turnout is lower, then, because citizens believe that elections have little connection to policy outcomes.

When control of the legislative and executive branches is divided between the two major parties, the effects of the separation of powers are exacerbated by the conflict between the two parties. Divided government has been the norm in American politics in the post–World War II era. Since 1952 there have been only eighteen years of unified control of government, and since 1972 there have been only eight years of unified control. Given the predominance of divided government, each cohort since the passage of the Twenty-Sixth Amendment entered in an era in which the separation of powers sent voters the message that elections were not linked to policy outcomes and thus they were socialized further to not vote. Younger voters, declining competition in elections, and divided government have played a key role in the turnout decline in the United States.

What, then, are the reasons behind lagging turnout in the United States, compared with other industrialized nations? Turnout in the United States was lower before the decline set in. In 1960, the last election before the decline began, turnout in the presidential election was 62.8 percent. In the other nineteen industrialized democracies referred to in this text the mean turnout rate for elections held in 1960 was 80.7 percent.[7] Although the decline in the United States appears to have widened the gap between it and other countries, the difference in 1960 illustrates the need to search for explanations to the low turnout in U.S. elections. Franklin's argument concerning the competitiveness of elections and the role of divided government in turnout highlights the role of institutions in shaping turnout. Using the work of Franklin (2004), Powell (1986), and Jackman (1987), the analysis in this book explores the impact of American electoral and governmental institutions on turnout.

The Turnout Puzzle

Why voting turnout is consistently lower in the United States than in comparable industrialized democracies is a pressing issue for several reasons. First, participation is the heart of democracy, and America prides itself as a birthplace of democracy and the leading proponent of the spread of democracy around the world. Why then are Americans laggard in going to the polls in their own democracy? Second, Americans' poor participation has a decided bias to it, with the poor, the less educated, and the young less likely to participate than the wealthy, the better educated, and the older. What factors help generate this participation gap? Third, while some have argued that governance is most effective when only the most engaged and informed citizens participate in the political process, the structures of government in the United States are based in part on the belief that widespread participation should be limited to prevent tyranny imposed by an uninformed majority. There is another side to this debate, however. Electoral participation is a matter of voice, of having a true say in the choosing of governmental leaders who craft policy that may have a dramatic impact on people's lives. Widespread participation creates greater democratic legitimacy because all groups in society have a say in choosing elected officials. Finally, citizen engagement in politics—or lack of it— is often taken as an index to the health of a democracy and public support for it. Are citizens turning out to vote at lower rates in the United States because of deep problems they have with their government—or for more mundane reasons?

In this book I argue that the primary explanation for the lower voter turnout in the United States lies with the nation's institutional arrangements: American electoral and governmental institutions increase the costs associated with voting, making it far more difficult than it is elsewhere. Consequently a large proportion of the eligible population refrains from voting, particularly those who are most likely to be disengaged from politics, such as the young and those of lower socioeconomic status. Although turnout may rise and fall for a variety of reasons, it is consistently lower in the United States because of institutional reasons. By and large, this lower turnout does not indicate greater citizen unhappiness with the government, as compared with citizens elsewhere; rather, it flows from the complex nature of the political institutions that constitute American democracy. This factor must be considered in evaluations of American democracy, including the tendency to undermine participation among the underclass.

While there are several institutional factors in the United States that complicate national turnout rates, the analysis in this book will focus on the three most consequential ones: (1) registration laws, (2) single-member district, winner-take-all elections, and (3) the separation of powers system. This institutionalist argument is developed in the following seven chapters. Chapter 2 presents the range of theoretical explanations for turnout, including the socioeconomic model, the cultural explanation, and the calculus of voting. It concludes by arguing that an institutional perspective on turnout is the most comprehensive explanation for the turnout differences between the United States and other established democracies.

Chapter 3 explores the impact of registration laws on turnout in the United States. By forcing citizens to take the initiative to vote and setting the time for registration, they increase the costs of registration and thus filter out all but those most likely to vote. Chapter 4 places the U.S. electoral system in context by discussing the various electoral systems used in democracies around the world. Chapters 5–6 examine the impact of single-member district, winner-take-all elections on turnout in the United States. Chapter 7 examines the impact of the separation of powers system on turnout. Chapter 8 concludes by examining the various methods that have a reasonable chance of leading to higher levels of turnout in the United States. These include moving to the proportional allocation of electoral votes in presidential elections, implementing Election Day registration at the national level, moving Election Day to the weekend, implementing early and mail-in voting on a national basis, and instituting public financing of congressional campaigns.

Notes

1. McDonald and Popkin (2001) argue that turnout in the United States is artificially low because the voting age population (turnout = votes per voting age population) includes individuals who are not eligible to vote, such as legal and illegal aliens and institutionalized citizens. The authors reestimate turnout using what they call the voting eligible population (VEP), which does not include ineligible persons, and conclude that turnout in American elections is, on average, about four percentage points higher than the artificially depressed rate using the voting age population (VAP). Even with this new measure, however, turnout in U.S. elections is still substantially lower than in most industrialized democracies. All of the data used in this paragraph are taken from Michael McDonald's website at http://elections.gmu.edu/voter_turnout.htm. The chapters in the book that examine the United States alone use the VEP, while chapters that compare the United States to other democracies use the VAP to calculate turnout.

2. Given that this book aims to explain turnout levels in the United States, comparing the United States to similar countries is necessary. While other

projects have used extensive lists of countries in comparative examinations of turnout (Blais 2000; Franklin 1996), I have chosen to include only stable, long-established democracies (Dahl 2002; Jackman 1987; Jackman and Miller 1995; Powell 1986). Using the standard employed by Jackman (1987) and Powell (1986) of countries that have been stable democracies since 1950, I choose twenty countries for analysis, taken from the list of countries used by Dahl (2002), Jackman (1987), and Powell (1986). See Appendix A for a list of the countries used in this text.

3. The mean turnout rates presented in Figure 1.1 are based on the voting age population rather than the voting eligible population. The U.S. data used in this chapter are taken from the Federal Elections Commission, and the international data are calculated from data supplied by the International Institute for Electoral Assistance at www.idea.int.

4. The mean turnout rate for industrialized democracies excludes Switzerland, which had a mean rate of 40.60 since 1960. Like the United States, Switzerland has unique institutional arrangements and is therefore generally considered an outlier.

5. The countries experiencing turnout increases are Malta, Sweden, Australia, Denmark, Norway, and Belgium.

6. McDonald and Popkin argue that turnout in fact has not declined; the apparent decline is a statistical artifact of the way we measure turnout—as actual votes cast per voting age population. Because the Census Bureau includes in its measure of the voting age population individuals who are not eligible to vote (incarcerated citizens and illegal and resident aliens), the measure is inflated and thus makes turnout appear lower than it is. Given that the proportion of illegal or resident aliens has grown dramatically over the past three decades, turnout would appear to decline, when in fact the measure of the voting age population is being artificially inflated (McDonald and Popkin 1999).

7. Some countries did not hold elections in 1960 and therefore data are taken from the election closest to 1960.

2

Explanations
of Turnout

A phenomenon as complex as national-level turnout cannot be explained with one simple variable or even one theoretical framework. In fact, there are several potential explanations for the differential turnout levels between the United States and other industrialized democracies. This book argues that the institutional explanation for the turnout problem in U.S. elections provides the most comprehensive explanation. But before discussing the institutional explanation in greater detail, I shall examine the various potential explanations for the turnout problem in the United States.

Socioeconomic Resources
and Turnout

Proponents of the socioeconomic status model argue that individuals with greater education, income, and occupational status vote at higher rates than those with less. To provide a comprehensive explanation of political participation in the United States, Verba, Schlozman, and Brady (1995) took the socioeconomic model and included it in a more comprehensive model, the civic volunteerism model. Their model includes three broad categories of predictors to explain why some people participate and others don't. First, individuals with resources of time, money, and civic skills are more likely to participate. People with free time are obviously more able to participate in politics than people without. People who have money make financial contributions to parties, candidates, and interest groups. Individuals with civic skills, such as language and organizational skills, are more likely to feel comfortable participating in politics and are more likely to be effective when they do. Civic skills can be acquired in a variety of ways, but in large part they come from occupations that require language and organizational skills, from membership in voluntary associations that teach and utilize these skills, and from formal education. The work of Verba and colleagues suggests that the pool of political participants to a large degree is composed of individuals from the middle and upper tiers of the socioeconomic ladder.

Although Verba and colleagues sought to explain all forms of political participation, their model is particularly applicable to turnout. For example, resources specifically and socioeconomic status broadly are strong predictors of turnout. Individuals with resources are much more likely to vote. A consistently powerful predictor of individual-level turnout is education. As noted above, education provides civic skills such as language and organizational skills, as well as the cognitive skills conducive to voting. The act of voting requires individuals to take in and process complicated information about the political world. Individuals with higher levels of education easily acquire and understand this information. Additionally, individuals with higher levels of education are more likely to understand how the electoral and governing system work and therefore more likely to understand the impact of government activity on their lives. Consequently educated individuals are more likely to be interested in and to follow electoral and governmental politics.

Income is also related to the probability of voting. People with money are more likely to vote (as well as engage in other forms of participation). Those with low income focus on obtaining the necessities of life rather than following politics and voting on Election Day (Rosenstone 1982; Wolfinger and Rosenstone 1980). Individuals with higher income are likely to live and work in an environment that is politically stimulating. Since they are exposed to political information on a daily basis, they are more likely to be interested in politics and thus more likely to vote (Conway 2000).[1]

Clearly socioeconomic status is a key predictor of individual-level voting probability.[2] However, if it is a key predictor of the difference in turnout between the United States and other industrialized democracies, then we must observe significant differences in socioeconomic level between the United States and other industrialized democracies. Powell (1986) found that during the 1970s the United States had the highest level of education (measured as the average years of education for adults over 25) of all the established democracies in his study. Additionally, the percentage of the workforce employed in white-collar occupations was much higher in the United States than in the other countries. He concludes that given the higher levels of these important predictors of participation, they cannot explain turnout differences between the United States and other nations.[3]

As noted above, economics can play a key role in turnout. For example, Rosenstone (1982) found that turnout is generally lower during economic downturns. Radcliff (1992) found the same pattern cross-nationally, but with an interesting twist. In developed nations, economic bad times resulted in lower turnout. However, in developing nations, economic downturns produced higher turnout. Radcliffe argues that the relative economic security provided by the welfare state in developed nations allows citizens to turn away from politics because they know that the state will provide their minimum necessities. In developing nations an economic crisis, in the absence of a welfare state, can literally affect the survival of families and thus participation becomes important. Radcliffe also argues that the marginal nature of the U.S. welfare state and the social stigma attached to welfare raise the costs of participation for marginalized citizens suffering economic distress; thus turnout is even lower than in other developed nations. All in all, the economics argument has only limited ability to explain the turnout difference between the United States and other industrialized democracies. If increasing economic output leads to increasing turnout, then one can reasonably assert that nations with higher levels of economic output should have higher levels of voter turnout. Given that the United States has greater economic output than most of the other established democracies considered in this text, it is unlikely that differences in economic impact can explain the turnout difference.[4]

Psychological Engagement and Turnout

The second component of the civic volunteerism model is a citizen's level of engagement with the political world. A citizen who is psychologically engaged with the political world is more likely to participate in politics (Conway 2000; Verba, Schlozman, and Brady 1995). Engagement is generally measured by variables that attempt to gauge citizens' (1) level of interest in politics, (2) level of political efficacy, (3) level of partisanship, and (4) level of information about the political world. Each variable gauges a citizen's degree of engagement with the political world, and each can serve as a strong predictor of electoral participation. For example, a citizen who states that he or she is interested in the current campaign or follows public affairs "most of the time" is clearly engaged with the political world. Individuals such as this have a very high probability of voting. Between 1964 and 2002 the mean reported vote for individuals with a high level of general interest in politics was 87.8 percent, while over the same period the mean reported vote for those with a low level of interest was 43.7 percent.[5] Clearly individuals who are interested in government and politics are more likely to vote in elections than are those with low levels of interest in politics.

Political efficacy also measures the degree to which an individual is connected to the political world. Efficacy is actually composed of two distinct dimensions. The first is internal efficacy, which measures an individual's self-perceived competence to effectively participate in politics; individuals who have a high level of internal efficacy, or believe they are capable of effectively participating in politics, are more likely to vote than those with a low level of internal efficacy (Craig, Niemi, and Silver 1990; Craig 1993). For example, internal efficacy can be measured by an individual's agreement with the statement that "politics is too complicated." Between 1964 and 2002, 84 percent of respondents who disagreed with the statement (indicating a sense of internal efficacy) reported voting, while 71 percent of those agreeing with the statement (indicating a low sense of internal efficacy) reported voting. Although not as dramatic a difference as we saw with interest in politics, the data do indicate that individuals who have a sense of internal efficacy are more likely to vote than those who don't.

External efficacy is the second dimension of political efficacy. It is generally defined as the degree to which a citizen believes that government is responsive to the needs and demands of the electorate (Craig, Niemi, and Silver 1990; Craig 1993). Individuals who believe this are likely to also believe that elections will result in policy outcomes and therefore are likely to vote (Franklin 1996; Franklin and Hirzcy 1998; Franklin 2004). The data from 1964 through 2002 support this contention; 84 percent of individuals scoring high on the external efficacy reported voting, while 60 percent of those with low levels of external efficacy voted. As expected, individuals who believe that government is responsive to the demands of the electorate are more likely to vote than those who do not.

Partisanship has been intensely studied by students of political behavior. Broadly defined as a long-term psychological attachment to one of the two major political parties (Campbell, Converse, Miller, and Stokes 1960), partisanship is a strong predictor of electoral participation (Abramson and Aldrich 1982). Between 1964 and 2002, 86 percent of strong partisans voted, 73 percent of weak partisans voted, 72 percent of independents who leaned toward one of the two major parties voted, but only 53 percent of individuals claiming to be pure independents voted. Those who lack attachment to one of the parties have a substantially lower probability of voting than individuals who claim at least minimal attachment to one of them.

The final attitudinal correlate of participation is knowledge of the political world. Individuals with a high degree of political knowledge are likely to be engaged and connected to the political world and thus more likely to vote. Eighty-four percent of those who could correctly identify the majority party in the House of Representatives between 1964 and 2002 reported voting, while only 58 percent of those who incorrectly identified the majority party in the House cast a ballot in an election. Clearly individuals with some knowledge of American politics are more likely to cast a ballot in an election than those who cannot demonstrate minimal knowledge.

Research exploring the relationship between citizen attitudes and political participation shows that citizens who are engaged with the political world are more likely to vote than citizens who are not engaged. One explanation suggests that the comparatively low turnout rates in the United States result from U.S. citizens being less engaged with politics and government affairs than citizens in other established democracies (Jackman 1987; Jackman and Miller 1995; Powell 1986). In effect, the American political culture is less conducive to electoral participation than the political cultures of other democracies. As defined in *Civic Culture* (Almond and Verba 1963), political culture refers to "attitudes toward the political system and its various parts, and attitudes toward the role of the self in the system" (p. 13). According to Almond and Verba, a nation's political culture is the allocation of orientations toward the political system among its citizens. We can identify the political culture of a nation by examining the attitudes that citizens hold toward the political system. If the United States has a political culture not conducive to participation, then we should be able to empirically demonstrate that American citizens have lower levels of important political attitudes such as interest in politics, internal and external efficacy, partisanship, and knowledge about the political world.

Based on their comparative analysis of five nations, Almond and Verba identified three broad types of political culture.[6] The first, *parochial,* is a culture in which most citizens are not connected to the political world. Government and politics are not part of citizens' lives and they have close to zero expectations of government activity. The second culture type, *subject,* is a polity in which citizens are aware of the political system and have attitudes about the legitimacy of the system; however, the citizens' orientation to the government is passive.

Citizens do not view participation as part of the system, and in many cases there may not be mechanisms for participation. The final political culture is the *participant* culture. Citizens in this culture are positively oriented toward the system and tend to take an activist view of politics, believing that participation is a necessary part of the process. Almond and Verba identified the United States as a participant culture, with citizens being highly engaged in politics and exhibiting high levels of political efficacy and partisanship. With a political culture that facilitates support of political institutions and participation in politics, it is unlikely that during the early 1960s, when the *Civic Culture* study was undertaken, the political culture of the United States could explain the lower level of turnout. While levels of important attitudes such as partisanship and efficacy declined in the United States during the 1960s and 1970s, they remained as high or higher than the mean levels of other democracies (Powell 1986). Powell (1986) estimated that if the other countries in his study had levels of political efficacy, partisanship, and interest in politics as high as the United States (i.e., if these countries had political cultures identical to that of the United States), turnout in these nations would *increase* by 3.12 percentage points.

Given the well discussed decline in civic engagement in the United States since the 1960s, it is possible that levels of these attitudes could have declined to levels lower than other industrialized democracies and thus turnout levels today could be in part a result of the long-term decline. In fact, levels of attitudes toward politics and government in the United States today remain as high or higher than levels in other industrialized democracies.[7] For example, in 2000, 56 percent of American respondents stated that they followed government and public affairs "some" or "most of the time." In 1999, 48 percent of European respondents stated they were either "somewhat" or "very" interested in politics. In terms of partisanship, Americans appear to more partisan than Europeans. Thirty-one percent of Americans claimed to be "strong partisans"; 55 percent are classified as either weak partisans (27 percent) or leaners (28 percent), and only 13 percent claimed to be pure independents or classified as apolitical. Only 7 percent of European respondents claimed to be "very close" to a political party, while 45 percent stated that they were either "fairly close" to a party (16 percent) or a party "sympathizer" (29 percent); 48 percent of European respondents stated that they were not close to a political party. Even if American leaners are combined with independents, the number of nonpartisans in the United States (41 percent) is still much lower than in Europe. Americans also appear to a bit more efficacious than Europeans. Sixty percent of Americans agree with the statement that "politics is too complicated," while 68 percent of Europeans agree with it. Comparisons of external efficacy are difficult in that different questions are used. In the European Election Study respondents are asked the degree to which they agree with the statement, "Parties and politicians in [name of your country] are more concerned with fighting each other than with furthering the common interest," and 84 percent agree that parties are more concerned with fighting among themselves than with promoting the common good. The closest question we can use in the United States is, "Public officials don't care much what people like me think," and only 31 percent of American respondents agree with that statement.[8]

The comparative data presented here should be viewed with caution. Each of the comparisons, with the exception of the "politics is too complicated" question, are based on different questions and thus some of the difference could result from differences in question wording. Additionally, Powell (1986) and Jackman (1987) used a set of countries that included five countries not in Europe—Australia, New Zealand, Japan, Canada, and Israel. The 1999 European Election Study includes Luxemburg, Portugal, and Greece, which the Powell and Jackman studies do not, and thus once again the differences highlighted above could be the result of the differences in the sample. It is unlikely, however, that the flaws noted would produce the differences highlighted above. Powell's findings about comparative levels of attitudes highlight the point that in order to explain the low turnout in the United States with the use of attitudes, one has to empirically identify lower levels of attitudes in the United States and other democracies. When the above data are examined in combination with the work of

Powell (1986) and Almond and Verba (1963), Americans appear to be as psychologically engaged as citizens in other countries and a bit more engaged. Based on this, attitudinal differences or the cultural argument can be safely ruled out as an explanation for turnout differences between the United States and other industrialized democracies. Jackman and Miller (1995) found that overall levels of life satisfaction, social trust, and political discussion had no significant effects on turnout in twenty-two industrialized democracies. The authors conclude that the findings of their project, taken in combination with previous work, indicate that political culture has no significant effect on cross-national differences in turnout.[9] Instead, the authors argue that institutional and electoral procedures such as registration and/or voting laws and the competitiveness of districts are the key determinants of turnout.

Mobilization and Turnout

The final component of the civic volunteerism model is recruitment or mobilization. Verba and colleagues argue that when individuals are recruited by political organizations and candidates to participate in politics, they are more likely to do so (Rosenstone and Hansen 1993). A large body of research indicates that when candidates, parties, and political organizations reach out to voters, turnout increases.[10] Mobilization efforts in the context of a campaign take place in various forms. The most common forms of get out the vote efforts (GOTV) are direct mail, telephone contact, and face-to-face canvassing. Each method is a direct attempt by a candidate, party, or political organization to directly contact a potential voter and get him or her to vote on Election Day. Gerber and Green (2000) found that face-to-face canvassing efforts had a strong impact on turnout rates, while direct mail efforts had a slightly positive effect on turnout, and telephone efforts appeared to have no effect. In large-scale elections such as state governor or U.S. senator or national presidential elections, most resources are used for media advertising to reach as much of the population as possible. Although the impact of negative campaigning on turnout rates is controversial, overall the evidence suggests that greater sums spent on television advertising lead to higher turnout rates (Freedman and Goldstein 1999; Goldstein and Freedman 2002; Hill and Mckee 2005).[11]

There is little dispute among students of political participation that mobilization efforts by candidates, parties, and allied groups lead to higher levels of turnout. Rosenstone and Hansen (1993) argue that mobilization efforts are successful at increasing turnout because they in effect subsidize the act of voting. In their efforts to win the support of potential voters, candidates and parties reduce the costs of participation by informing voters when, where, and how to vote, notifying them of upcoming rallies and visits by candidates, and even providing transportation to the polls on Election Day. Mobilization increases turnout because it makes the act of voting easier for many citizens. Mobilization efforts likely increase the perceived importance of the campaign among citizens. Citing literature on blood drives and recycling efforts, Gerber and Green (2000) argue that face-to-face mobilization efforts increase the importance of participating and emphasize the "obligation to act." Greater levels of campaign advertising politicize the information environment for citizens and thus raise interest in a campaign, which would then lead to higher levels of turnout (Bullock, Gaddie, and Ferrington 2002; Jackson 1997).

Mobilization is obviously a key to turnout levels. In order to explain the turnout difference between the United States and other industrialized democracies, mobilization efforts would have to be lower or less effective in the United States than in other countries. Rosenstone and Hansen (1993) argue that a key cause of turnout decline in the United States since 1960 is a decrease in the level of mobilization. Gerber and Green (2000) mirror this argument by stating that the decline in turnout reflects the decline in face-to-face turnout since the 1960s. Mobilization efforts are a key part of the argument presented in this book and thus we will return to the effect of mobilization on turnout in the United States later in this chapter.

A Note on Rational Choice

One of the more well-known and controversial theories in political science is the calculus of voting. First posited by Anthony Downs in *An Economic Theory of Democracy* (1957), the theory can be expressed by the following formula:

$$R = (PB){-}C$$

Where R is the total utility, or benefit, that a citizen receives from the act of voting; B is the benefit the citizen receives from his preferred candidate winning the election instead of the less preferred candidate; P is the citizen's expectation that her vote will be decisive in determining the outcome of the election; and C is the cost of the act of voting to the citizen (Downs 1957; Riker and Ordeshook 1968).[12] The core argument of the theory is that voters must calculate before casting a ballot the overall benefit they expect to receive from voting versus the costs of voting. If the benefits outweigh the costs, then citizens will most likely vote. If the benefits are outweighed by the costs, then citizens will most likely not vote. In order to determine this, each citizen must perform a simple calculus to determine whether or not to vote. The citizen must first decide what benefit he will receive if his preferred candidate wins versus the less preferred candidate: this is the B term in the formula. If the difference in benefit is large, then the potential benefit of voting is great. If the difference is small or none, then the potential benefit approaches zero (Downs 1957; Riker and Ordeshook 1968; Blais 2000). As Blais (2000) notes, it is not the potential benefit that is important but rather the expected benefit that the voter perceives she will receive. Therefore, the P term in the formula represents the citizen's perception that her vote will be decisive in determining the outcome of the election. P is dependent, then, on (1) the closeness of the election and (2) the size of the electorate. If an election is close, it is reasonable to assume that a citizen perceives his vote is important. However, if the election is not competitive, then the citizen is not likely to believe his vote is crucial. The size of the electorate is also relevant. In small-scale electorates a close election is likely to convince a potential voter that her vote can make a difference in the outcome of the election, and in order for her preferred candidate to win she must vote. In contrast, in large-scale national elections, the probability of a single vote being decisive is almost nil, and therefore most citizens will conclude that their vote won't matter. Given that in the calculus formula B is multiplied times P, the product will almost always be small. In national elections the perceived benefit will normally approach zero, and therefore the citizen should conclude that he will receive very little benefit if his candidate wins.

After assessing the expected benefit of his candidate winning, the citizen then must determine if the costs associated with voting are larger or smaller than the benefit. These costs are registration (in the United States and France), the actual time it takes to vote, and the time and effort expended to acquire information concerning the candidates, parties, and issues involved in the election. As noted earlier, if these costs outweigh the expected benefit, it is unlikely that a citizen will vote. Given that the expected benefit will in most cases be small (due to the large size of electorates), the costs associated with voting will always outweigh the benefits and thus the formula suggests it is "irrational" to vote.

Of course countless people do vote. The average turnout rate for industrialized democracies approaches 80 percent, and even in the United States turnout rates in presidential elections have averaged 54 percent since 1960. Because of this, we are left with the "paradox of voting." Most people vote even though it seems irrational to do so, at least based on the original formula; many scholars have attempted to amend the theory in order to "rescue" it and bring it more in line with the reality of turnout rates. These include the belief that voting is essential to maintain democracy; individuals vote out of a sense of duty; citizens vote because they don't want to regret not voting if their candidate loses by one vote; people vote because they believe others won't vote and thus their vote could be crucial; politicians and groups make it easier for citizens to vote (reduce the costs); citizens vote because the costs associated with voting are so small they are not substantially greater than the benefits received; finally, most individuals find it rational to not calculate the costs and benefits associated with voting because both are so small.[13]

All of the above amendments have been challenged and debated. Most are probably partially correct, and none can completely salvage the theory's ability to predict turnout. Aldrich (1993) argues that the calculus of voting has been interpreted too narrowly. It is not the closeness of the election that prompts citizens to vote because their vote will make a difference; rather, politicians seek to win votes through campaign efforts and thus induce citizens to engage in an activity that will bring them little direct benefit but will cost them very little.[14] Blais notes that while the calculus of voting is limited in its ability to empirically predict whether or not an individual will vote, it is a useful tool in helping explain turnout. For example, the formula gives us three variables that should impact turnout. First, citizens are more likely to vote when they perceive that they will receive a benefit from their preferred candidate winning (B). We can therefore try to identify factors that might cause differences between the United States and other democracies in the perceived benefit of a citizen's preferred candidate winning. Second, while it is unlikely that an individual citizen's vote will ever determine the outcome of an election (P), we do know that the closer an election, the higher the turnout level (Cox and Munger 1989; Jackson 1996; Blais 2000). Because of the established relationship between closeness and turnout, we can search for factors that might cause American elections to be less competitive than elections in other countries. Finally, while the costs of voting are relatively low, increases in the costs of voting would likely lead to decreases in turnout; therefore we can look for differences in the costs of voting between the United States and other democracies.

The analysis in the remainder of this book will rely on the calculus as an analytical tool. Because it is not my goal to test the calculus of voting, I do not attempt to empirically verify its predictive ability, nor does the analysis I present in the following chapters rely on formal models to examine differences in turnout. Instead, this book is informed by the calculus of voting. When appropriate, I will interpret the findings of the analysis through the framework of the calculus of voting. For example, the overall argument in this book is that the electoral and government institutional arrangements of the American system create an environment which constrains rather than facilitates turnout by (1) influencing the competitiveness of elections and (2) increasing the costs associated with voting. The remainder of this chapter will examine the impact of institutions on turnout.

The Role of Institutions in Shaping Turnout

Cross-national research suggests that differences in electoral and government institutions appear to be the key factors in explaining turnout differences across countries (Powell 1986; Jackman 1987; Jackman and Miller 1995; Franklin 1996, 2004). Consequently any effort to provide an in-depth analysis of low turnout in the United States must focus on the role of institutional arrangements in shaping turnout. Before turning to a discussion of the research on the impact of institutions, we will consider what institutions are and why they affect human behaviors such as voting.

Institutions can be thought of humanly created constraints that influence and structure human behavior. These constraints can be formal, such as rules, laws, and constitutions, or they can be informal, such as norms or conventions of behavior (Crawford and Ostrom 1995). From the institutionalist perspective, all human behavior occurs within an institutional context or environment, and the activities of individuals and collectives of individuals can be explained, in large part, by interaction between the individual and the institutional setting in which the individual exists (March and Olson 1989). In terms of political institutions, then, this refers to the formal rules, laws, and constitutions that define governments, elections, and so on. Examples of political institutions are legislatures and parliaments, administrative agencies, constitutions; rules governing access to the ballot such as registration laws; rules governing the nature of elections and representation such as single-member district winner-take-all elections, proportional representation, the Electoral College, and the actual structure of governments such as the separation of powers or parliamentary governments.

As noted by March and Olsen (1989), "political institutions define the framework within which politics takes place" (p. 18), and thus individual choices and actions within this framework are shaped by the rules set forth by the institution. For example, the U.S. House of Representatives is an institution defined by the Constitution and rules written by the House itself throughout its history. Although members have changed the institution of the House over time, in large part the choices made by congressional members at any given time are influenced by existing institutional structures of the House. The voting behavior of citizens in a polity is governed by the rules that determine access to the ballot, representation in government, and to some degree the structure of government itself. Consequently, while we can use individual characteristics such as demographics and attitudes toward the government to explain differences in the probability of voting between individuals within the same country, we must remember that all citizens within a polity exist within the same institutional context. Consequently, other factors, such as demographic characteristics, come to the fore in influencing turnout.[15] Also, demographic differences in turnout and even attitudinal differences are likely determined by the institutional context. For instance, state-level registration laws are rules that control access to voting process. They determine when and how a person registers to vote, and anyone who wants to vote in an election must fulfill the requirements set forth by the state law. By increasing the costs of voting, registration laws are believed to have their greatest impact on the young, those of lower socioeconomic status, and recent movers (Highton 2004). To explain turnout in the United States, then, we need to move past an examination of individual-level characteristics and examine differences in the institutional arrangements that govern individual political behavior.

There are several pieces of research that examine the impact of institutions on turnout from a cross-national perspective. The goal of this text is to build on these works by taking their overall findings and using them to examine the role of institutions in the United States. Collectively, this body of research has identified two groups of institutions that impact turnout: (1) electoral laws and (2) governmental institutions. Electoral laws define the legal context in which voting takes place. They determine who can vote by controlling access to the voting process. The most examined electoral law in relation to turnout is voluntary registration. In the United States (as well as France) it is up to the individual citizen to place her name on the list of citizens eligible to vote. In contrast, most industrialized democracies have a system of automatic registration in which the responsibility for placing citizens on the list of eligible voters rests with the government. Powell (1986) estimated that if the United States were to implement a system of automatic registration, turnout would increase as much as fourteen percentage points. Compulsory voting is also known to produce higher levels of turnout. Jackman (1987) found that in nations that mandate voting by law, turnout was on average thirteen percentage points higher than nations without compulsory voting.[16] Registration and voting laws are a key component of turnout in the United States. We will consider the impact of registration laws on turnout in Chapter 3.

The nature of electoral competition is a key predictor of turnout. We have already established that close elections bring citizens to the polls, and in part this is most likely based on the belief that in close elections every vote counts. However, competitive elections also prompt parties and candidates to reach out to voters in an attempt to gain their support. Powell (1986), Jackman (1987), and Jackman and Miller (1995) found that in nations with districts that were competitive at the national level, turnout was higher than in single-member district systems. In nationally competitive districts, parties mobilized voters all over the nation in an attempt to win the election. In single-member district systems, on the other hand, some districts will be competitive, while others will be uncompetitive. Parties and candidates with limited resources will only spend them in competitive districts in which the outcome is uncertain. Turnout is lower, then, in single-member districts because intense mobilization occurs in a relatively few competitive districts while in systems with nationally competitive district mobilization takes place over the entire country. Jackman estimated that nationally competitive districts increase turnout by about fourteen percentage points.[17] In Chapters 5–6 we will take an in-depth look at the impact of single-member district, winner-take-all elections on competition turnout in U.S. congressional and presidential elections.

Powell (1986) included in his analysis a measure of party group linkages, which gauges the linkage between political parties and social groups. This measure indicates the degree to which parties within a polity are closely linked with particular social groups. For instance, if workers in manual labor jobs overwhelmingly support a socialist or communist party, while white-collar workers support a conservative or pro-business party, then this country would score relatively high on the party-group linkage measure. The United States has traditionally scored very low on the party group linkage score; according to Powell, at the time of his study the United States had one of the lowest group linkage scores of the countries in his study. Powell argues that close linkages between parties and social groups lead to higher turnout because "partisan choice should seem simpler to the less involved; cues from the personal environment of the individual (friends, family, and coworkers) should be more consistent; party organizers can more easily identify their potential supporters in making appeals and helping voters to the polls on Election Day (Powell 1986, 22)."

From this perspective, then, close linkages between parties and social groups reduce the costs of participation for voters by creating an environment in which most of an individual's associates support the same party and thus provide the potential voters with consistent cues about politics. Additionally, close linkages between parties and groups reduce the costs of mobilization for parties, since a party closely linked with a given social group knows exactly who its supporters are and where to find them. Powell estimated that if the average democracy had the U.S. level of party group linkages, turnout would decline by over ten percentage points; and if the United States had European levels of party-group linkages, turnout would increase in the United States by about ten percentage points.[18]

Several governmental institutional factors have been identified as key predictors of national-level turnout. Disproportionality indicates the degree to which the percentage of votes won in an election are translated into actual seats in a legislative body. Jackman (1987) found that disproportionality in vote translation reduced turnout. Systems that allocate seats in the parliament proportionate to a party's share of the vote have higher turnout than systems that allocate seats disproportionately. The U.S. system of single-member district winner-take-all elections is disproportional; even if a congressional candidate loses with 49.9 percent of the vote, she will not receive a share of the seats in Congress, while in a proportional system a party receiving 49.9 percent receives approximately 50 percent of the seats in the parliament. Jackman found that controlling for other institutional factors, truly proportional systems had turnout levels about nine percentage points higher than truly disproportional systems. Jackman also found that multiparty systems have lower levels of turnout—because the voter has no true role in selecting the government due the necessity of coalition formation in multiparty systems. The voter is simply voting for a party that will then participate in the selection of the government. In contrast, unicameralism (legislature is composed of one chamber) leads to higher levels of turnout because the legislative body, unlike the U.S. Senate and House of Representatives, does not have to compete to pass policy. In these systems, then, citizens are able to choose governments that can be more decisive in policymaking. Jackman estimated that two-party systems (such as the United States) had turnout levels about twelve points higher than true multiparty systems, while unicameral systems had turnout levels about eight points higher than bicameral systems.[19]

The final institution found to have an impact on turnout is the actual structure of government. Franklin (2004) argues that separation of powers systems (e.g., the United States) should have lower levels of turnout because the government is less responsive to the wishes of the electorate. Franklin identifies executive responsiveness, which he defines as "the extent to which the complexion of the executive is responsive to the choices made at the time of an election" (Franklin 2004, 96), as a key institutional factor influencing national-level turnout.[20] The idea here is that voters decide which party they want to control government and thus the set of policies they want to be enacted. Systems in which the legislative branch controls the nature and policies of the executive are capable of easily translating the electorate's wishes into policy. In our separation of powers system the legislative branch is elected separately from the executive and therefore has no control over who inhabits the executive branch. While the legislative branch may have some control over the policies enacted by the executive (all laws must be passed by Congress), the president can veto any law passed by Congress. Given this arrangement, our governmental system is less responsive to citizen demands (in fact it was designed to be less responsive), and according to Franklin citizens believe that elections are not linked to policy outcomes and turnout is lower because elections are viewed as unimportant. Accountability, or simply the ability to assess the performance of the government, is also lower in separation of powers systems, as each branch can blame the other for policy failures, scandals, and so on. The reduced ability to assess government performance increases the information costs for many citizens, and turnout should be lower in more accountable systems such as parliamentary systems.

The separation of powers is also vulnerable to divided control of government, in which control of the executive and legislative branches are divided between the two parties. In fact, in the post–World War II era divided control of the federal government has been the norm. During periods of divided government, responsiveness and accountability should be reduced even further, given that control of the executive and legislative branches is divided between the two major parties. Because of this, information costs are increased and citizens should be more likely to believe that elections are not very important and turnout should consequently be lower than periods of unified control of government. Chapter 7 focuses on the impact of divided government on citizen attitudes toward government and turnout.

The extant research on cross-national turnout indicates forcefully that the causes of turnout differences across polities are mainly institutional. The remainder of this book explores this literature and builds on it by focusing on the impact that registration laws, single-member district, winner-take-all elections, and the separation of powers make on turnout in American elections.[21]

Notes

1. See also Leighley and Nagler 1992; Martinez and Hill 1999; Wolfinger and Rosenstone 1980; Rosenstone and Hansen 1993.

2. Other factors strongly related to political participation and voting are age (Conway 2000; Wolfinger and Rosenstone 1980; Highton and Wolfinger 2001) and race (Verba et al. 1995; Hill and Leighley 1999).

3. Powell's study used data from the 1960s and 1970s. Using data from the 2005 U.N. *Human Development Report*, the numbers remain relatively the same. The average number of years of education for adults over the age of 25 in the United States is 12, while in the other nations considered in this book the mean years of education for adults is 9.8.

4. Only Denmark, Ireland, Norway, and Switzerland have higher gross domestic products (measured in 2003 U.S. dollars) than the United States. United Nations Department of Economic and Social Affairs, Statistics Division, http://unstats.un.org/unsd/demographic/products/socind/inc-eco.htm.

5. The figures presented here and in the rest of this section were calculated using data from the 1948–2002 National Election Study cumulative file. Any opinions, findings, conclusions, or recommendations expressed in these materials are those of the author and do not necessarily reflect those of the National Science Foundation or the University of Michigan.

The self-reported vote in surveys is always inflated due to misreporting on the part of respondents (Burden 2000, Martinez 2003), and thus the data presented in this section should be viewed with that caveat in mind. The purpose of using the data in this section is to empirically demonstrate the well-established relationships discussed in this section.

6. The countries analyzed in *Civic Culture* were the United States, Great Britain, Germany, Mexico, and Italy.

7. The data used here are taken from the 2000 National Election Study and 1999 European Election Study. See Appendix B for the questions used from both surveys.

8. There were no comparable questions in the 1999 European Election Study that would allow a comparison of political knowledge between Europeans and Americans.

9. Powell 1986; Jackman 1987.

10. See Caldiera, Patterson, and Markko 1985; Cox and Munger 1989; Wielhouwer and Lockerbie 1994; Rosenstone and Hansen 1993; Hill and Leighley 1993, 1996, 1999; Jackson 1996, 1997; Gerber and Green 2000, 2001; Hill and Mckee 2005.

11. The effect of television advertising on turnout is hotly debated, however, largely centering on whether negative advertising depresses turnout, stimulates turnout, or has no effect. Early work (mainly in the form of experiments) on the topic found that exposure to negative campaign ads reduced the likelihood that an individual would cast a ballot in an upcoming election (Ansolabehere et al. 1994; Ansolabehere and Iyengar 1995; Ansolabehere, Iyengar, and Simon 1999). Recently several researchers found that rather than depressing turnout, negative advertising stimulates turnout or has no significant effect (Clinton and Lapinski 2004; Finkel and Geer 1998; Freedman and Goldstein 1999; Goldstein and Freedman 2002; Kahn and Kenney 1999; Wattenberg and Brians 1999).

12. For the remainder of this text I will use male and female pronouns interchangeably.

13. The above summary was taken from Andre Blais's thorough and impressive examination of the calculus of voting, *To Vote or Not to Vote: The Limits and Merits of Rational Choice Theory.*

14. See also Jackman 1993.

15. In the American system of federalism, institutions vary somewhat across states. For example, state laws governing registration procedures vary and thus turnout levels vary.

16. In 1993 Italy eliminated compulsory voting and turnout did not decline. While not conclusive, this does suggest compulsory voting is not the dominating influence on turnout some think it to be (Franklin 2004).

17. Using a different model specification, Powell (1986) found that if the average democracy had the competition level of American single-member districts, turnout would decrease by about three percentage points.

18. Powell also noted that the frequency with which the executive changed hands between parties affected turnout; nations in which control of the executive changed frequently witnessed higher turnout. In this regard, the United States is advantaged compared to other established democracies.

19. The United States and Switzerland, the two countries with the lowest turnout, have one key factor in common: both hold elections frequently and thus citizens are called on to participate in elections on a regular basis. Some have argued that in these countries many voters suffer from "voting fatigue" and feel overwhelmed with the sheer number of elections. Franklin (2004) found that across time the frequency of elections has no significant impact on national level turnout.

20. See also Powell 2000.

21. The analysis presented in this book excludes proportional representation (it is discussed in Chapter 5), multipartyism, unicameralism, compulsory voting, and party-group linkages. Each of these must be done with comparative analysis, and given that U.S. institutional arrangements are unique in the world, the analysis in this book relies solely on an examination of the effect of institutions in the United States, although supplementary comparative analysis is provided where appropriate.

3

Restricting Access
to the Ballot Box

The Impact of
Registration Laws on Turnout

Among all of the institutional features of the American system, registration laws have the greatest impact on overall turnout levels in the United States (Powell 1986). Other institutional factors such as single-member districts and the separation of powers impact turnout by creating an environment that discourages turnout through shaping the mobilization efforts of the candidates and parties (winner-take-all elections) or impacting citizen attitudes toward government (separation of powers). Registration laws, on the other hand, constrain turnout by restricting citizen access to the voting booth. In this chapter we will examine the impact of registration laws on turnout, beginning with an overview of the history of the registration requirement in the United States.

The History of Voting Restrictions
in the United States

As Kleppner (1982) notes, the Constitution expressly delegates the power to designate voter eligibility requirements to the states, while reserving to Congress the right to alter voter eligibility requirements. Because each state determines who can and cannot vote, the inclusiveness of electoral politics varies throughout the country. States have placed requirements on voting, ranging from property and tax requirements in the early days of the republic, to citizenship requirements in response to the wave of European immigrants in the mid-nineteenth century, to the legal exclusion of African Americans through Jim Crow laws following the end of Reconstruction (Lane 1959; Kleppner 1983; Piven and Cloward 2000). By the beginning of the twentieth century, requiring individuals to place their name on the list of registered citizens before being allowed to vote had become the central form of voter eligibility requirement in states outside the South. By 1920 thirty-one nonsouthern states had some type of personal registration requirement in place, although as with most eligibility requirements the strength of the law varied from state to state (Kleppner 1982).[1] By 1929 only Arkansas, Texas, and Indiana had not instituted registration procedures, although they eventually did so (Piven and Cloward 2000).

Piven and Cloward (2000) have argued that officials imposed registration requirements to selectively shape the composition of the electorate and thus played a key role in the demobilization of the working class and minorities in the early part of the twentieth century. Although the registration requirement gave local officials the ability to restrict access to the ballot box to certain groups, it also grew out of the belief among Progressives that some type of control over the electoral process was needed to prevent widespread voting fraud (Rusk 1970; Converse 1972). Lengthy residency requirements (a citizen must live in a state for a specified period of time), proof of residence, and registration at one centralized location such as a town hall or county jail were intended to ensure that would-be voters were legitimate state citizens.

Whether or not registration laws effectively reduced voting fraud, the personal registration requirement shifted responsibility for establishing a citizen's eligibility to vote from the state to the citizen. The costs of participation rose dramatically and turnout dropped during this period. While there is disagreement as to the exact impact of registration requirements on turnout during this period, Kleppner (1982) estimates that in counties with stringent registration requirements turnout declined approximately 30 percent. The decline in turnout was not evenly distributed across socioeconomic categories, however. The increase in the costs of electoral participation skewed the electorate toward those most engaged with politics and therefore most likely to overcome the barrier of the registration requirement (Kleppner 1982). Individuals who were only marginally engaged with the political world but might be mobilized in the later days of the campaign were unable to do so because they were not on the registration lists. The long-term impact, then, of the registration innovation was to create an electorate composed of those most likely to participate in elections and to exclude those unwilling or unable to overcome these barriers (Kleppner 1982).

There were four major adjustments to the legal structure of participation during the twentieth century: the Nineteenth Amendment provided suffrage to women, the Twenty-Fourth Amendment eliminated poll taxes, the Voting Rights Act of 1965 eliminated discriminatory registration laws, and the Twenty-Sixth Amendment provided suffrage to eighteen- to twenty-year-olds. However, the system of registration requirements in the states remained in place. While all citizens were guaranteed the right to participate in elections, they had to first place their name on the list of citizens registered to vote. As part of the Voting Rights Act Amendments of 1970, Congress limited the length of time a state could shut off the opportunity to register to thirty days as well as the time requirements for state residency prior to registration (42 U.S.C. 1973, A–1). Both of these limits were later upheld by Supreme Court rulings.[2]

The 1970s witnessed state-led experimentation with improving access to the ballot box. The best-known reform was the Michigan motor voter program implemented in 1975. The secretary of state, Richard Austin, implemented a program that included having office staff prompt citizens to register when they visited the driver's license bureau (Knack 1995; Rhine 1995; Solop and Wonders 1995). Wisconsin began making registration applications available in public agency offices, such as AFDC and food stamp offices, as early as 1973 (Solop and Wonders 1995). Both California and Phvania followed Wisconsin's

lead by making registration applications available in public agency offices, but clients were not asked whether they wanted to register. By the
end of the 1970s, four states had some form of "convenient" agency-
based program in place.

During the 1970s other forms of convenient registration reforms
were implemented by various states. North Dakota eliminated the registration requirement in 1973, and between 1972 and 1976 Maine, Minnesota, and Wisconsin adopted Election Day registration (EDR):
citizens were allowed to register to vote on the day of the election (Fenster 1994; Solop and Wonders 1995). In 1977, as part of a package of
electoral reforms, President Carter proposed the Universal Voter Registration Act, which sought to make Election Day registration mandatory
in all states. Citing the increased likelihood of fraud and the imposition
of federal programs on states, Republican opponents killed the bill in
the House and Senate. Two other states implemented EDR programs
during the 1970s. The one in Ohio was defeated by a citizen referendum
in 1977. Oregon had an EDR program prior to the Carter proposal, but
it was eliminated in 1986 by a constitutional amendment (Smith 1977).
As of today, the reform has never been successfully implemented at the
federal level, and only six states have EDR programs as of this writing.

Texas implemented the nation's first mail-in registration program
in 1941 (Solop and Wonders 1995), and during the 1970s twenty other
states implemented programs that allowed citizens to register to vote
through the mail. As with most state reforms, the restrictiveness of
these mail-in programs varied from state to state. Some states required
the citizen to do nothing more than fill out the application and mail it
back, while other states required the application to include notarized
verification of identification (Highton and Wolfinger 1998; Knack
1995). By 1993 and the passage of the National Voter Registration Act
(NVRA), thirty-two states had implemented mail-in registration programs (Knack 1995).

From Movement to Federal Law

The National Voter Registration Act was arguably the most comprehensive electoral reform since the Voting Rights Act of 1965. The re-

form, better known as "motor voter," addressed the registration requirement by mandating all states that did not have Election Day registration (and North Dakota, which does not have registration) to
allow citizens to register to vote at driver's license offices, through the
mail, and at public agencies such as TANF (Temporary Assistance for
Needy Families) and unemployment offices. The law was the result of
eighteen years of state experimentation with various reforms attempting to make it easier for U.S. citizens to register and vote.

As already noted, Michigan implemented the nation's first motor
voter program in 1975. By 1982 a handful of other states had implemented the reform. In 1983 academics Frances Fox Piven and Richard
Cloward published an article in *Social Policy* calling for a "class-based realignment" (Piven and Cloward 1983). They argued that "two-thirds of
the disenfranchised" (Moss 1993) were poor and low-income Americans, and the most effective way to counter the policies of the Reagan
administration was to mobilize this group of citizens where they were
easiest to contact: social service agencies. This would be aided by the
tendency of most social service professionals to be supportive of human
service programs and thus likely to help all efforts, with the intention of
saving the social welfare state (Piven and Cloward 1983; Moss 1993).

Human Serve, a nonprofit organization formed by Richard A.
Cloward and Frances Fox Piven in 1983 to advocate for expanded
voter registration, enlisted the support of prominent associations such
as Planned Parenthood, the YWCA, public employee unions, and professional social work unions. Unfortunately the complexity of coordi-
nating a multiplicity of different agencies and the sensitive political
nature of trying to mobilize particular sectors of society created a
range of implementation problems. By the end of 1984, over 1,500
agencies that offered clients registration opportunities had added only
275,000 people to the registration rolls (Moss 1993).

Compounding the difficulty of establishing an agency-based registration movement was the fact that even if agencies offered the opportunity to register, there were still state registration laws to adhere to,
such as lengthy residency requirements and lengthy closing dates. This
nationally oriented movement therefore had to work within the myr-
iad registration laws across the federal system. Human Serve and its

supporters used the federal system to its advantage. Rather than attempting to mobilize the social service community, the group turned its attention to institutional reform. Initially the movement sought out sympathetic governors, mayors, and county officials to issue executive orders mandating that workers in government agencies offer clients the opportunity to register. This plan won endorsement from the National Association of Secretaries of State and the National League of Cities (Moss 1993).

Friendly governors in major states like Texas, Ohio, and New York signed executive orders establishing agency-based programs. The impact of these orders was diluted by the Reagan administration's threat to cut aid to any state that used these funds to pay employees engaged in registration activities. These three states continued to offer registration at public agencies by making the registration application available in office space, rather than prompting the client whether or not she wanted to register (Moss 1993). Nonetheless, the idea of convenient agency-based registration grew in popularity, and in the late 1980s a series of state legislatures controlled by Democrats passed motor voter laws similar to Michigan's (Moss 1993). By 1987 nine states (AK, AZ, CO, MI, NC, OH, PA, VT, and WA) had implemented motor vehicle registration programs in which office staff asked clients whether or not they wanted to register to vote (Knack 1995).

In 1988 the move toward a comprehensive national registration law entered the halls of Congress. In April and May 1988 the House of Representatives held hearings to consider bills proposing the national implementation of mail-in registration, Election Day registration, and registration in government and private sector agencies (Solop and Wonders 1995).[3] While there was substantial support for the reform in both houses, the NVRA remained stalled in Congress from 1989 to 1991 as a result of two successful filibusters by Senate Republicans. Republican opponents argued that if passed and implemented, the reform would impose unnecessary burdens on the states and open the door to voting fraud.

In 1992 the reform was passed by both the House and Senate after a Republican-led filibuster was defeated; the bill was vetoed by President

Bush, who cited the same concerns as congressional Republicans about an increased burden on states and voting fraud.

The prospects for implementation improved in 1992 with the election of Bill Clinton as the forty-second president of the United States. One plank of Clinton's policy agenda was to expand voter registration opportunities, and the 1992 Democratic Party platform included a provision calling for new laws to expand the electorate. Clinton pledged to sign the same law Bush vetoed in 1992 (Solop and Wonders 1995). Once elected, President Clinton signaled Congress to send him a voter registration bill, and one of the first bills considered by the 103rd House of Representatives was HR–2: National Voter Registration Act of 1993 (Solop and Wonders 1995). After overcoming filibuster efforts by Senate Republicans, the reform was presented to President Clinton, and on May 20, 1993, he signed the National Voter Registration Act, a law almost identical to the one vetoed by President Bush a year earlier. All states affected by the law were required to implement the provisions of the NVRA by January 1, 1995. States that had to amend their constitution to implement the law were given until January 1, 1996 (Solop and Wonders 1995). The law required all states not having Election Day registration and North Dakota, which does not require registration, to allow citizens to register to vote when they acquired or renewed their driver's license, through the mail, or at public agencies such as AFDC, food stamps, unemployment, and so on.[4] The reform also prohibited states from removing citizens from registration lists for nonvoting (PL 103–31.1993).

In remarks given when signing the bill into law, President Clinton stated that the key to increasing electoral participation in the United States is reduce the barriers to registration:

> . . . the failure to register is the primary reason given by eligible citizens for their not voting. The principle behind this legislation is clear. Voting should be about discerning the will of the majority, not about testing the administrative capacity of a citizen. (Solop and Wonders 1995, 79)

With this statement President Clinton spelled out the logic of most who supported the reform. Individuals from low participation groups such as the poor and less educated refrained from participating in elections because the obstacle of registration was too burdensome to overcome. The key to increasing participation rates, then, was to make registration as easy as possible.

The Impact of
Registration Laws on Turnout

As already noted, registration laws are a key factor in explaining differences in turnout between the United States and other democracies.[5] The United States has a system of voluntary registration based on the individual citizen traveling to a government location to register or placing her name on the registration list through the mail or online. In contrast, most other democracies have a system of automatic registration in which the government places the citizen's name on the registration list when he reaches voting age. And some nations have compulsory registration laws that require citizens to place their name on the list of registered citizens. Additionally, several nations have voting laws that compel citizen to vote in elections (Powell 1986; IDEA 2002).

Figure 3.1 presents the mean turnout rates from 1960 through 2001 for selected industrialized democracies.[6] Not surprisingly, nations with compulsory voting laws have high voting rates, with a mean turnout rate of 87 percent. Nations with automatic registration have a mean turnout rate of 76 percent, while the two voluntary registration countries, France and the United States, have substantially lower rates of 65 percent and 55 percent respectively. The data in Figure 3.1 show that the voluntary registration requirement works to depress turnout.

Rosenstone and Wolfinger (1978) estimated that a complete liberalization of registration laws in the United States would result in a nine percentage point increase in overall turnout. Similarly, Powell (1986) found that if automatic registration were implemented in all states, overall turnout in U.S. presidential elections would increase by ten

FIG 3.1   Comparative Turnout by Voting Laws, 1960–2001

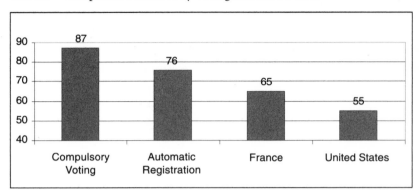

Source: International Institute for Democracy and Electoral Assistance; Federal Elections Commission

percentage points. The impact of the registration requirement on turnout is easily explained. While electoral participation is a relatively low-cost activity, requiring citizens to take the initiative to place their names on the list of registered citizens increases the costs of voting. Thus many citizens are unable or choose not to overcome this obstacle, while those who want to participate in elections (i.e., those who are engaged with the political world) will overcome this obstacle. In effect, citizens who are engaged with the political world register because they want to vote. Erikson (1981) argued that the individual who voluntarily places his or her name on the list of registered voters is "investing" in the act of voting. The purpose behind registering is to enable to the individual to vote in the next election, and because of this turnout among registered voters tends to be high. For instance, between 1980 and 2000, 85 percent of registered voters cast ballots in presidential elections.[7]

Erikson's argument is based on the notion that registration laws affect electoral participation in the United States by "selecting" those most likely to vote. Mitchell and Wlezien (1995) built on this perspective by arguing that in order to gain a clear understanding of the impact of registration laws on the American electorate we must first look at how registration laws shape the size and composition of the registered electorate and then examine the impact on the size and composition of the voting electorate. The authors found that a complete relaxation of registration laws in the United States would increase the size of the registered population by approximately nine percentage points. This increase would raise overall turnout by approximately eight percentage points. A complete relaxation of registration laws would increase the proportion of individuals with lower levels of education in the registered electorate, but the composition of the voting electorate would remain relatively unchanged.[8]

Restrictive registration requirements, then, appear to impact turnout levels by restricting the size of the registered electorate. Brown, Jackson, and Wright (1999) argued that states with restrictive registration requirements tend to have a smaller proportion of their eligible population registered to vote than states with less restrictive registration requirements. These states have fewer voters eligible to vote on Election Day and thus have lower turnout than states with more relaxed procedures. Figure 3.2 illustrates the impact of restrictive registration procedures on the size of the registered and voting populations between 1980 and 1992. Recall that prior to the implementation of the NVRA in 1993, states already had a variety of convenient registration programs in place: Election Day registration,[9] pre-NVRA reforms[10] (motor vehicle registration or mail-in program), and no pre-NVRA reforms.[11] The two states with Election Day registration (Maine and Minnesota) had almost universal registration, with 99 percent of the eligible population registered to vote.[12] In states with either active motor vehicle programs or mail-in registration programs, 80 percent of the eligible population was registered to vote, and states with no convenient registration had the lowest registration level, 75 percent, of their eligible population registered to vote. The easier the registration method, the more individuals registered to vote.

As mentioned earlier, Jackson and colleagues argued that states with restrictive registration procedures would have smaller registered populations (Figure 3.2) and thus fewer citizens eligible to vote on Elec-

FIG 3.2   Registration and Turnout by Ease of Registration, 1980–1992

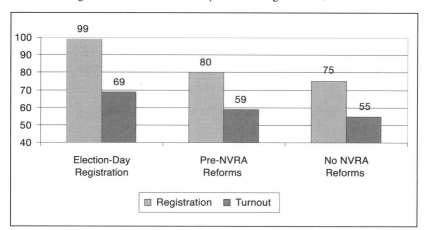

Source: Federal Elections Commission

tion Day, resulting in a lower turnout rate. This can be seen in Figure 3.2, which shows the mean turnout rates of these three categories of states. Election Day registration states had the highest level of turnout, an average of 69 percent of the eligible population voting on Election Day.[13] This reflects nearly universal registration as well as the ability of nonregistered citizens to show up on Election Day, register to vote, and then cast a ballot. The states with motor vehicle and/or mail-in registration programs in place had an average turnout of 59 percent, and states with no program had a mean turnout rate of 55 percent. Figure 3.2 appears to support the argument by Brown and colleagues that restrictive registration requirements constrain the size of the registered population and thus constrain turnout because there are fewer eligible citizens eligible to vote on Election Day.

Registration and Social Groups

State registration laws reduce the size of the registered electorate and thus by extension reduce the size of the voting population. The work on the impact of registration laws also suggests that restrictive registration requirements have their greatest impact on disadvantaged groups such as those with lower levels of income and education (Campbell et al. 1960; Rosenstone and Wolfinger 1978; Wolfinger and Rosenstone 1980; Mitchell and Wlezien 1995). The impact on disadvantaged groups is fairly easy to explain. Voluntary registration depends on the resources and motivations of the individual (Erikson 1981; Jackson 1996). Because voluntary registration is a relatively burdensome task that must be fulfilled in most cases at a time prior to the election (in most states thirty days) and thus takes place before the campaign peaks, individuals who are not engaged with the political world are less likely to register than those who are engaged. The registered population tends to be skewed toward Americans who are older and have higher levels of education and income. These groups are more likely to place their name on a list of registered voters as an "investment" in the act of voting (Erikson 1981; Jackson 1996; Timpone 1998).

Table 3.1 presents the proportion of citizens of given social groupings (education, income, age, race/ethnicity, and length of residence) registered to vote between 1980 and 1992 across the three classifications of registration (Election Day registration, motor vehicle and/or mail-in registration, no reforms). The first pattern of note in the table is that across all three forms of registration individuals with higher socioeconomic status (education and income), older Americans, and whites register in greater proportions than individuals of lower status, younger Americans, and racial/ethnic minorities. The differential impact of the registration requirement on different social groupings can be examined by comparing the proportion of individuals from the bottom and top of a social grouping (e.g., less than high school diploma vs. bachelor's degree or higher) across the three registration classifications.

If voluntary registration has a greater impact on lower-status groups, then we would expect the difference in the proportion of top and bottom group members registered to vote to be greater in both voluntary registration classification (pre-NVRA reforms and no reform) than in the Election Day registration states. While gaps still exist between those of lowest levels of education and income and those from the highest in the Election Day registration states, the gaps are much smaller than either the pre-NVRA reform or no-reform states. For instance, the difference in registration between individuals without a high school diploma and those with a college degree in Election Day registration states is seventeen percentage points, while in states with either mail-in or motor vehicle programs the difference is thirty-two percentage points and in states with no reforms in place the difference is twenty-seven percentage points. Although the gaps between those with those with the lowest and highest levels of income are smaller across all three classifications, the gaps are smaller in the EDR states (14 percentage points) than in the voluntary states (24 percentage points in the pre-NVRA reform group and 18 percentage points in the no-reform group).

The pattern is the same for age and racial and ethnic groupings. The difference in the proportion of the oldest age groups (65 and above) and the youngest (18–29) is much smaller in EDR states (3 percentage points) than in reform states (23 percentage points) and the no reform states (24 percentage points). Interestingly, among racial/ethnic groups, the gaps between whites and blacks (8 points) in the EDR states is almost identical to the voluntary registration states, while the gaps between whites and Hispanics (22 percentage points) is much larger in the EDR states than in reform or no-reform states.

Based on the data presented in Table 3.1, we can see that the requirement of registering at a specified period of time prior to an election appears to filter out individuals from lower-status groups who are less likely to be engaged with the political world. The result of this is a registered electorate skewed toward higher education, income, education groups, and white citizens. The gaps between privileged and nonprivileged groups are no smaller in the pre-NVRA reform states than in the no-reform states (in some cases they are larger), suggesting that reforms which leave the voluntary nature of registration in place do little to bring lower-status individuals into the registered electorate.

TABLE 3.1   Percentage of Individuals Registered to Vote by Social Grouping, 1980–1992

	Election Day	Pre-NVRA Reforms	No VRA Reforms
Less than High School	79	58	62
High School	85	65	68
Some College	89	76	78
Bachelor and Above	96	90	90
Bottom 20%	78	59	66
Second 20%	84	66	68
Third 20%	82	71	72
Fourth 20%	91	76	78
Top 20%	92	83	84
18–29	78	58	59
30–45	90	74	74
46–64	92	81	82
65 and Above	91	81	83
White	88	75	76
African-American	80	68	69
Latino	66	65	63
Less than two years	83	60	58
More than two years	92	78	79

Source: Current Population Survey: Voter Supplemental File: 1980, 1984, 1988, 1992

Squire, Wolfinger, and Glass (1987) argue that registration laws have their greatest impact on individuals who have recently moved, since every time a citizen changes address he must change his registration status. For many individuals, updating their registration status is not very high on the list of priorities related to a move. Furthermore, registration requirements virtually guarantee that individuals who move with some frequency and are only marginally connected to the political world will not register to vote. The final two rows in Table 3.1 clearly illustrate the impact of registration on movers. The gap in registration between those who have lived at their current address for less than two years and those resident for more than two years is nine percentage points in EDR states, eighteen percentage points in pre-NVRA reform states, and twenty-one percentage points in no-reform states. The more difficult the registration requirement the larger the gap between those who have moved recently and those who have not.

As the above discussion notes, the pool of citizens eligible to vote on Election Day is skewed toward individuals from certain social groups. Consequently, if every registered citizen participated on Election Day, these gaps between privileged and nonprivileged groups would be translated into the voting population, which would be as skewed as the registered population. The only way the voting population could become more balanced would be for registered citizens from the lower-status groups to participate at higher rates than higher-status groups. In fact, while the gaps between higher- and lower-status groups are substantially reduced among voters, given that 85 percent of registered citizens cast ballots, individuals of higher status still participate at higher rates than lower-status individuals. Table 3.2 presents the gaps in voting between the highest and lowest groups for education, income, age, racial/ethnic, and length of residence groupings. Substantial gaps between privileged and nonprivileged groups exist across all classifications. Among education groups, for instance, the difference in turnout between individuals with less than a high school education and those with a bachelor's degree or higher is fifteen points in the EDR states, thirteen points in the pre-NVRA reform states, and twelve points in the no-reform states. Interestingly, gaps in the EDR states appear to be larger than in the voluntary registration states, although with the exception of racial and ethnic groups they are similar. We would expect to see little difference in voting across registration classifications because registration laws have their impact on registration and not voting among registered citizens. Given that the pool of registered voters is already skewed toward privileged groups and that registered individuals from privileged groups vote at higher rates than individuals from nonprivileged groups, the voting population in the United States tends to be substantially skewed toward higher SES groups, older Americans, whites, and and those who don't change residence frequently.[14]

TABLE 3.2   Difference in Voting Between the Top and Bottom of Social
Groupings, 1980–1992

	Election Day	Pre-NVRA Reform	No NVRA Reform
Less than High School/College	15	13	12
Bottom 20%/Top 20%	17	13	14
18–29/65 and Above	5	6	7
White/Black	14	6	5
White/Hispanic	14	10	3
< Two years/>Two years	5	5	6

Source: Current Population Survey: Voter Supplemental File: 1980, 1984, 1988, 1992

The Impact of Implementing the NVRA
and Election Day Registration in the 1990s

As already noted, the NVRA was signed into law in 1993, and implementation was to be complete by January 1, 1995.[15] The logic of the
reform is simple. Making the opportunity to register available to as
many citizens as possible should expand the registered electorate and
turnout should rise, given the increased number of potential voters eligible to vote. Supporters also argued that the increased ease of registration would bring marginalized groups such as the young, the poor,
and racial minorities into the registered and voting populations. The
most ardent and optimistic supporters argued that reform would
bring about large increases in turnout (Piven and Cloward 1983,
1996), while other observers were more cautious. Highton and Wolfinger (1998), for instance, argued that the law would have its greatest impact on those who had recently moved and was unlikely to have a great
impact on overall turnout. Based on an examination of states with
NVRA-type programs prior to the implementation of the federal law
in 1995, Knack (1995) concluded that the driver's license provision of
the reform was likely to have a greater impact on registration and
turnout levels than either the mail-in or public agency provisions of
the law.

While the reform has only been in effect since 1995 (ten years at this writing), several studies have attempted to determine whether or not the law has had its intended effect. Martinez and Hill (1999) found that in the 1996 election, states that moved from having no NVRA provisions to implementing the federally mandated programs experienced no change in overall turnout levels. Interestingly, the authors found that the tendency of the voting electorate to be skewed toward those with higher levels of education was modestly exacerbated. Knack (1999) found no evidence to suggest that the reform did anything to alleviate the tendency of whites and middle to high SES groups to participate at greater rates than racial minorities and individuals from lower SES groups. Knack's work did suggest, however, that the reform appeared to close the voting gap between older and younger Americans.

Wolfinger and Hoffman (2001) examined the impact of the reform on the registered and voting populations and found that in 1996 the implementation of motor vehicle provisions had little impact on registered or voting populations. In fact, individuals from higher education and income groups, older Americans, and whites all had a higher probability of registering at these locations than individuals from low-participation groups. Public agency registration was successful at registering racial minorities and individuals from low socioeconomic groups. However, public agency registrants, as well as motor vehicle registrants, had a lower probability of voting once registered than individuals who registered at more traditional locations such as a town hall or an election office. Hill (2003), on the other hand, found that changes in the socioeconomic and age composition of the registered electorate were evident in 1998, with greater numbers of individuals from lower education and income groups and young Americans registered under the new law. Hill also found that the reform appeared to modestly reduce the tendency of the voting electorate to be composed of individuals from higher socioeconomic and age groups. However, that impact was realized in an indirect way. Changes in the voting electorate were the product of changes in the registered population, although the effects of the law were greater on the composition of the registered electorate than the voting electorate.

The reform's greater impact on registration than on voting is easily illustrated. Between 1980 and 1992 states with neither motor vehicle nor mail-in programs on average had 75 percent of their voting eligible population registered to vote (Fig. 3.2). Between 1996 and 2000, following the implementation of federal reform, the proportion of the eligible population registered increased to 81 percent (Fig. 3.3). Compare this to states that had motor vehicle or mail-in programs prior to the implementation of the NVRA. The percentage of registered voters in these states between 1980 and 1992 was 80 percent (Fig. 3.2), which increased to 84 percent following the implementation of the national law registration (Fig. 3.3). Although the size of the registered population increased in both states, states moving from no programs in place to the federally mandated motor vehicle, mail-in, and public agency appeared to experience modestly larger increases in the proportion of eligible population registered to vote than states with programs already in place.

As noted, there was no impact on overall turnout levels. The average turnout in states with reforms in place between 1980 and 1992 was 59 percent (Fig. 3.2), and in states with no reform in place turnout was 55 percent (Fig. 3.2). Following the implementation of the NVRA, turnout in pre-NVRA reform states between 1996 and 2000 was 55 percent (Fig. 3.3), and turnout in no-reform states was 52 percent (Fig. 3.3). Even after the implementation of a substantial registration reform and a subsequent increase in the proportion of citizens registered to vote, the gap in turnout between these two groups of states was only reduced by one percentage point. This lack of impact on turnout is easy to explain. As mentioned, voting in the United States is a two-step process: the potential voter is required to register and then vote in an election. By making registration more convenient, the NVRA appears to have created a modestly larger and more representative registered electorate. However, the reform does nothing to motivate the newly registered citizen to vote in the next election. Whatever individual-level obstacles (e.g., socioeconomic resources or personal attitudes) existed prior to registration still stand between the citizen and the voting booth. Therefore, when an individual registers for the first time

FIG 3.3   Registration and Turnout by Ease of Registration, 1996–2000

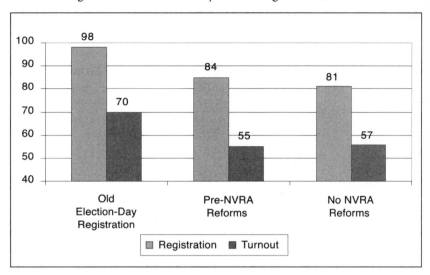

Source: Federal Elections Commission

under NVRA procedures, it is highly unlikely that she will cast a ballot in a future election unless she possesses the resources and attitudes conducive to electoral participation. However, individuals who register under the new procedures and do possess resources and attitudes conducive to participation are more likely to vote. Consequently the NVRA is likely to make the act of registration (and thus voting) easier for those individuals predisposed to electoral participation.

Although the initial impact of the NVRA appears modest, the Hill project suggests a lag effect (no impact in 1996 but a significant impact in 1998). This is consistent with Knack's (1995) study of states with motor voter reforms prior to the implementation of the national law. He found that the longer a state had a motor voter program in place the greater the proportion of individuals registered to vote and the higher the overall level of turnout. Because motor vehicle registration is based on providing the opportunity to register to individuals who are acquiring or renewing licenses, we would expect that the longer a motor vehicle program is in place the more individuals will be registered under the law (Knack 1995, 1999). While the NVRA will never substantially increase turnout or eliminate the bias in American electoral politics toward advantaged groups, the work of Knack (1995) and Hill (2003) indicate that as time goes by and more people register under the reform, the registered population should increase and turnout should increase modestly as well.

Election Day Registration

One reform that most students of participation agree could have a substantial impact on turnout is Election Day registration. Six states have it in place as of this writing, and as shown in Tables 3.1-3.3, EDR states have higher levels of registration and turnout than states without EDR (Fenster 1994; Highton 1997; Brians and Grofman 2001). Even after the implementation of NVRA reforms, citizens must register during a specified period of time before the election. Most states have closing dates of thirty days, which means election officials close off registration after that date, and no individual can register for the upcoming election after that date. Wolfinger and Rosenstone (1980) identified the closing date as having the largest impact on voting of all registration restrictions on turnout. The closing date works to depress turnout because states are closing off the opportunity to register just as the intensity and visibility of the campaign has the potential to engage peripheral voters (Jackson 1996; Brians and Grofman 2001). Election Day registration eliminates the closing date and thus provides an opportunity for voters who become engaged late in the campaign to register and vote on Election Day.

As mentioned, six states (ID, ME, MN, NH, WI, WY) have Election Day registration, and registration and turnout levels in these states are higher on average than in states without Election Day registration. Idaho, New Hampshire, and Wyoming implemented EDR programs in the early 1990s instead of NVRA procedures. Therefore, we must examine registration and turnout in these states between 1980 and 1992 and then in 1996 and 2000 in order to determine what impact, if any, the implementation of these programs had on registration and turnout levels. Figure 3.4 looks at registration and turnout rates across four state classifications (old EDR, new EDR, pre-NVRA reforms, no reform) in 1996 and 2000. The mean level of registration in the three new EDR states between 1996 and 2000 is 81 percent. This is similar to states that did not have EDR prior to 1992 and substantially lower than the three old EDR states (98 percent). Mean turnout in the new EDR states during this time was 61 percent, which is substantially lower than the 69 percent turnout rate in the old EDR states but higher than the other states without EDR. To confidently judge the impact of implementing EDR on registration and turnout rates, we need to look at registration and turnout levels in these three states prior to 1992. The registration rate in new EDR states between 1980 and 1992 (prior to the implementation of EDR) was 81 percent, and mean turnout over this time period was 61 percent. These numbers are identical to the registration and turnout rates for these states between 1996 and 2000, suggesting that this reform had no impact on registration and turnout rates. While the data here provide no clear explanations for the lack of impact, it is possible that as time goes by these numbers will increase as the programs become more institutionalized.

The data used in this book preclude the examination of registration and turnout rates in old EDR states prior to implementation, as all three states implemented programs between 1973 and 1976. The three new EDR states had higher levels of registration and turnout than other states prior to the implementation of the reform. Registration and turnout in the original EDR states was likely higher than the rest of the country as well. Brians and Grofman (2001) use longitudinal data from 1972 through 1996 to control for prior levels of turnout, and they also control for a variety of factors known to influence turnout. They find that EDR implementation resulted in about a seven percentage point increase in turnout. Brians and Grofman's work suggests that the implementation of EDR does lead to increased turnout.

There is also evidence to suggest that EDR may bring marginal groups into the voting population. Highton (1997) found that in North

FIG 3.4   Registration and Turnout by Ease of Registration, 1996–2000

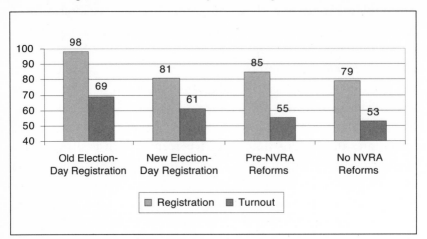

Source: Federal Elections Commission

Dakota (no registration) and the three old EDR states the gap in turnout between age and education groups was lower, as well as the gap between those who had lived at their current address for less than a year and those who had lived there for more than three years. Brians and Grofman (2001) found that EDR implementation had the greatest impact on individuals of middle socioeconomic status (high school education and middle income), although the impact is almost equally strong for those of lower SES. At this point no data suggest that EDR does or does not have an impact on the different voting rates among racial groups. The work of Brians and Grofman (2001) and Highton (1997) suggest that the implementation of Election Day registration would bring about higher levels of turnout and a modestly more representative electorate.

Conclusion

The discussion and data presented in this chapter suggest that registration requirements in the United States constrain electoral participation by making voting a two-step process: the individual must first place his or her name on the list of citizens registered to vote before being allowed to cast a ballot in an election. The registration requirement appears to "filter out" individuals who are modestly engaged or not engaged at all with the political world. Because of this, the registered population is constrained in size and tends to be skewed toward individuals most likely to vote—those with higher levels of education and income, older Americans, and those who have not moved recently. As a result of the smaller and "biased" registered population, overall turnout tends to be low and also skewed toward individuals identified above, those with higher levels of education and income, older Americans, and those with a stable residence.

Recent reforms such as the NVRA appear to have limited impact on overall electoral participation. While the NVRA appears to have created a modestly larger and more representative registered electorate, it has had limited impact on turnout. However, as more people register under the new reform, the registered population should increase and turnout should also increase as a result of the larger registered population. The limited impact of the reform is likely a function of the fact that the reform only makes registration easier; it leaves the voluntary nature of registration in place. Additionally, most states still have lengthy closing dates which shut off access to registration (and therefore the voting booth) just as most campaigns are reaching their greatest visibility.

The reform with most promise for bringing about increased turnout is Election Day registration, although the discussion and data in this chapter suggest its impact will also be limited. As Powell (1986) notes, even if automatic registration were uniformly implemented across the United States, turnout would only increase by about ten percentage points, which leaves it substantially lower than most other industrialized nations. Because of the limited impact of registration reform, we must look for other institutional factors behind the low turnout in U.S. elections.

Notes

1. Personal registration was not a new idea in 1920. Massachusetts had a registration requirement in 1800, and many states experimented with this

type of requirement throughout the nineteenth century (Piven and Cloward 2000).

2. *Oregon v. Mitchell* (1970).

3. The Election Day registration provision of the NVRA proved controversial and was taken out of the bill in committee deliberations in order to bring the bill to the floor for consideration.

4. Idaho, New Hampshire, and Wyoming implemented Election Day registration rather than NVRA procedures.

5. Because the McDonald and Popkin data for the voting eligible population start in 1980, all data, with the exception of the comparative data in Figure 3.1, are limited to the 1980–2000 period. The data were acquired from the Inter-University Consortium for Political and Social Research at the University of Michigan. Any opinions, findings, conclusions, or recommendations expressed in these materials are those of the author and do not necessarily reflect those of the National Science Foundation or the University of Michigan.

6. Compulsory voting nations are Australia, Belgium, and Italy; compulsory registration nations are Australia and New Zealand; automatic registration nations are Austria, Canada, Denmark, Finland, Germany, Ireland, Israel, Japan, Netherlands, Norway, Sweden, Switzerland, and the United Kingdom. France and the United States have voluntary registration.

7. The data for this calculation were taken from the 1980, 1984, 1988, 1992, 1996, and 2000 Current Population Survey, Voter Supplemental Files.

8. Mitchell and Wlezien also found that relaxation of registration laws would have no impact on the income and racial composition of either the registered or voting populations.

9. Maine, Minnesota, and Wisconsin adopted Election Day registration between 1972 and 1976. North Dakota is excluded from this analysis because it has no registration requirement. However, the mean level of turnout in North Dakota between 1980 and 2000 is 63 percent, substantially higher than voluntary registration states but lower than the Election Day registration states.

10. The following states either had a motor vehicle or a mail-in program (or both) prior to 1993: AK, AZ, CA, CO, CT, DC, DE, HI, IA, ID, IL, KS, KY, LA, MD, MI, MO, MS, MT, NC, NE, NH, NJ, NM, NY, NV, OH, OR, PA, RI, SC, SD, TX, TN, UT, VT, WA, and WV.

11. The following states had no registration reform in place prior to 1993: AL, AR, FL, GA, IN, MA, OK, VA, and WY. While ten states made registration available at public agencies such as AFDC and unemployment offices prior to the NVRA, only Minnesota had a program that prompted clients to indicate

whether or not they wanted to register to vote, and the effectiveness of these programs is not clear (Knack 1995). Because of this they are not considered part of the pre-NVRA reform group. Additionally, no state had a public agency program that did not have Election Day registration or motor vehicle or mail-in program. The classification of prior NVRA reforms and EDR are taken from Knack (1995).

12. This excludes Wisconsin because it does not keep records on the percentage of citizens registered to vote.

13. Includes Wisconsin.

14. This pattern is also evident in North Dakota. The gaps between privileged and nonprivileged groups in the state are similar to those in voluntary registration states, which suggests that easing registration requirements does little to mobilize those from lower-status groups.

15. Seven states (CA, IL, KS, PA, SC, VA, and VT) delayed implementation of the NVRA (Knack 1999).

4

Placing the
United States in Context

A Comparative Look at Electoral Systems

In Chapter 3 we examined the impact of registration laws on the turnout rate in U.S. elections. In this chapter and the two following ones we will examine the impact of the U.S. electoral system on turnout. Electoral systems are rules of the game that determine how votes are cast in a country's elections and how those votes are translated into governmental power (Blais and Massicotte 1996; Rae 1967). There are two main types of electoral systems in industrialized democracies. Plurality or majority systems seek to form a government that represents the preferences of the majority, or at least most of the citizens, within a country. Given this goal, they have been accurately classified as majoritarian systems. Proportional representation (PR) systems, on the other hand, attempt to form a government that is representative of as many groups in society as possible (Blais and Massicotte 1996; Lijphart 1984; Powell 2000).

The most common form of majoritarian system is the simple plurality rules election (or first past the post), in which the candidate or party with the most votes (not necessarily a majority, or 50 percent plus one vote) wins the election. Most plurality systems are based on single-member district elections (SMD) in which a nation, state, or region is broken into geographical districts, with each district electing

59

one representative to government. The main idea behind SMD is to elect a candidate who best represents the desires of most voters in each district. The second type of majoritarian system is based on majority rules. In these systems a candidate or party is required to win 50 percent plus one vote of the total vote in order to gain representation in the government (Dahl 2002; Blais and Massicotte 1996; Lijphart 1984; Powell 2000; Rae 1967). There are two variants of majority systems. The two-round system employs a second round, or *runoff* election, between the top two contenders if no candidate wins an outright majority in the first round of voting. The winner between the two candidates in the runoff election wins the seat in government (Lijphart 1984). The second type of majority system is the *alternative vote* (AV). Voters are required to rank their preferences among the candidates for office, and a candidate who wins a majority of first preferences wins the seat in government. However, if no candidate wins an outright majority, the candidate with fewest first preferences is dropped and ballots with this candidate listed as first preference are transferred to remaining contestants. This process of excluding the candidate with the fewest first-preference ballots continues until a true majority winner is identified (Blais and Massicotte 1996; Lijphart 1984; Powell 2000).

Proportional systems differ greatly from majoritarian systems, which place a single representative elected by a plurality or majority of citizens in government. PR systems allocate governmental power among political parties roughly proportional to their support among the electorate (Blais and Massicotte 1996; Dahl 2002; Lijphart 1984; Powell 2000; Rae 1967). There are two main types of PR systems used by industrialized democracies. The most widely used is the *list* system. Parties nominate a list of candidates either in one national (usually called at-large) district or in geographic districts with multiple representatives (called multimember districts). The seats in the legislature are then allocated based on the percentage of the vote a party receives from the electorate. For example, a party that wins 10 percent of the votes in an election will receive close to 10 percent of the seats in the legislature. The exact percentage of seats allocated in the legislature is determined by one of several formulas, which are beyond the scope of this discussion. In order for a party to actually be given seats in the legislature it must meet a minimum percentage threshold, for instance, 5 percent of the total vote (Blais and Massicotte 1996; Lijphart 1984; Powell 2000; Rae 1967).

The second type of proportional system is the *single-transferable vote* (STV). The voter casts a ballot for a single candidate rather than a list of candidates representing a party. This system is similar to the alternative-vote system in that the voter is asked to rank order his preferences among candidates. However, there are substantial differences between the two systems. First, the STV takes place in a multimember district. Second, a quota, or percentage of first preferences required to win a seat, is calculated (Blais and Massicotte 1996). All candidates meeting or exceeding this quota are given a seat in the legislature. Any first-preference ballots for this candidate that exceed the quota (surpluses) are then transferred to the other candidates based on second preferences. If all first preferences are transferred and seats remain unallocated, then the weakest candidate is eliminated and her votes are transferred to the other candidates. This process continues until all seats are filled (Blais and Massicotte 1996; Lijphart 1984; Powell 2000; Rae 1967). The main goal of PR systems is to ensure fair representation of both majorities and minorities and to avoid overrepresenting or underrepresenting any group (Blais and Massicotte 1996; Lijphart 1984; Powell 2000; Rae 1967).

Not all democracies fit neatly into one these categories. There are many variations of proportional representation, and many countries mix majoritarian and PR election methods. Some systems mix the two by using majoritarian and PR elections in different regions of the country. Other countries have mixed systems in which one set of legislative members is elected by majoritarian rules and one set by PR. Finally, some countries use PR to correct the disadvantage to small parties, which do not fare well in SMD elections (Blais and Massicotte 1996).[1]

The U.S. plurality system is mixed in that it uses three different methods at the national level, and some states and localities use multimember districts (Gerber, Morton, and Reitz 1998). In this chapter we will focus on national elections. Three separate and distinct elections are held on the national level: one for the presidency, one for the Senate, and one for the House of Representatives. The Senate is unique in that each state is treated as a multimember district with two representatives. However, there are separate elections for each seat (in most cases held in different years), and the elections are based on plurality rules. House of Representative elections are SMD in its pure form. Each of the 435 House districts is represented by one individual elected based on plurality rules. Finally, the president is elected through the unique Electoral College (EC). In the EC system we hold fifty-one separate plurality elections (one for each state and the District of Columbia), and the winner in each state is awarded the total number of electoral votes *(bloc vote)* allotted to that state (the total number of U.S. House and Senate members). There are two exceptions to the winner-take-all nature of the EC. Both Maine and Nebraska allocate electoral votes based on congressional representation. Thus the plurality winner in each congressional district is awarded one electoral vote, and the winner of the overall state vote is awarded two electoral votes, or one for each senator.

A Brief History of SMD
in the United States

The method of representation for the Senate and the Electoral College was written into the Constitution. However, the SMD election of the House of Representatives was not part of the Constitution. The only mention of House representation in the Constitution is that state representation in the House will be based on state population size and that the number of representatives will be equal to one per 30,000 citizens (today the ratio is one per 600,000 citizens). This is not to say that the framers didn't believe that SMD was the most appropriate form of representation. In Federalist Papers 56 and 57 James Madison refers to congressional members representing a district of a set number of citizens (Madison 1961a, b). Alexander Hamilton maintained that "the natural and proper mode of holding elections will be to divide the state into districts in proportion to the number to be elected" (Syrett and Cook 1961, 41). In the end, however, the Constitution set the broad parameters of representation for the House of Representatives and left the details of how representatives would be elected to the states.

In the years following the ratification of the Constitution states varied in how they elected House members. Five states used single-member districts and six states used at-large elections in which the total delegation was elected by and represented the entire state; Georgia and Maryland used a combination of at-large and district elections. By 1842 the union was composed of twenty-six states, ten of which chose their House delegation through at-large elections (*CQ Guide to United States Elections*, 729–738). During the congressional session in 1842, an amendment to mandate that states elect their House delegations through single-member districts was added to an apportionment bill. Despite vigorous objections over the constitutional right of the Congress to pass such a law, the amendment was passed. In defiance of the new law, four states (NH, GA, MS, and MO) held at-large elections with no response from the federal government or the courts (*CQ Guide to United States Elections*, 734–735). The lack of response by the federal government rendered the mandate impotent, and in 1850 the district mandate was dropped. In the decades that followed Congress passed districting mandates on six occasions (1862, 1872, 1882, 1891, 1901, and 1911), all with little or no effect. Although the majority of states chose to elect the representatives through district elections, a handful of states used at-large elections into the early twentieth century. It wasn't until 1967 and the passage of the last SMD district mandate that all fifty states elected representatives through the use of SMD elections.

Electoral Systems and Turnout

Given that electoral systems structure the nature of voting and how votes are translated into governmental power, it is reasonable to think that variations in turnout across nations should, in part, be a result of

FIG 4.1   Turnout Comparison Between Proportional and Single-Member District Systems, 1960–2000

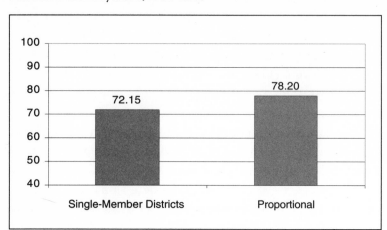

Source: International Institute for Electoral Assistance;
Federal Elections Commission

the different forms of electoral systems (Jackman 1987). In the remainder of this chapter, we will focus closely on the effect that plurality systems (SMD in particular) have on turnout. When compared to PR systems, plurality systems tend to have lower levels of turnout (Fig. 4.1).[2] Between 1960 and 2000 countries with PR systems had an average turnout of 78.20 percent.[3] In contrast, plurality systems had a much lower turnout rate of 72.15 percent over the same period.[4]

The data presented in Figure 4.1 are consistent with most previous research exploring cross-national variations in turnout. Most studies have found that PR systems have modestly higher levels of turnout than plurality or majority systems (Crewe 1981; Franklin 1996; Jackman 1987; Jackman and Miller 1995; Blais 2000; Blais and Carty 1990). The reasons for this pattern are not clear; however, most students of participation believe that in highly proportional systems there are fewer wasted votes—citizens who vote for minor parties are likely to receive representation in government. In contrast, supporters of minority parties in plurality systems who actually cast votes for a smaller party are not likely to receive representation in government, since these parties cannot win in systems in which the top vote-getter receives the seat in government. Consequently, many potential supporters of minority parties in plurality systems choose to abstain rather than cast a wasted ballot (Blais 2000; Franklin 1996; Jackman 1987).

In a perfectly proportional system each party would receive a share of seats in parliament in exact proportion to its share of votes in the election. Clearly PR systems are substantially more proportional than plurality systems. However, some PR systems translate votes more proportionally than others, and thus we can think of proportionality as a continuum ranging from very disproportional plurality systems to the most proportional of the PR systems. The greater the degree of proportionality the higher the degree of turnout (Blais 2000; Franklin 1996; Jackman 1987; Jackman and Miller 1995). Blais (2000) notes that disproportionality has little to no effect on turnout in non-PR systems, and thus the effect is mainly in the differences in proportionality among PR systems. Blais found that turnout in a purely PR system would be about six points higher than in a non-PR system. However, when the proportionality differences among PR systems are taken into account, this difference is reduced somewhat. As Lijphart (1984) notes, no system is perfectly proportional.

In any discussion of plurality and PR systems it is important to discuss the impact each has on the number of political parties in a country. In 1951 political scientist Maurice Durverger posited that plurality systems would favor the creation and maintenance of a two-party system. He went so far as to say that the effect is close to being a "sociological law," or a phenomenon that will always occur given certain conditions. In this case, where plurality systems are in place, we will find an electoral system dominated by two parties. This phenomenon has been known ever since as "Durverger's law." Durverger's argument is fairly straightforward. He explains the pattern in terms of a mechanical effect and a psychological effect. The mechanical effect is that minor parties are underrepresented in the party system because they usually lose elections in each district in a plurality systems. The psychological effect is that voters come to realize that minority parties cannot win an election and consequently vote for the major party that is closest to them ideologically (Blais and Carty 1991; Durverger 1954; Riker 1986; Taapagera and Shugart 1989). Similarly, party elites come to realize that forming a small party that cannot win a plurality election is a waste of finite resources (Blais and Carty 1991). Across time, there is a reinforcing relationship in which voters won't support minor parties that can't win and elites won't form minor parties that can't win; in this way the dominance of the two major parties is strengthened. In contrast, PR systems do not impose such constraints on minority parties, and PR usually produces a vibrant multiple party system.

Many people argue that the lack of choices in the two-party system in the United States is a central cause of low turnout. They point to the high turnout rates in PR systems and conclude that the existence of multiple parties in a PR system leads to higher turnout because voters have more choice. Although it seems counterintuitive (at least from the perspective noted above), the greater the number of parties in an electoral system the *lower* the turnout (Jackman 1987; Jackman and Miller 1995). This pattern is relatively easy to explain. Elections in a multiparty system are less important because voters are not directly choosing government; rather, they vote for party that will form a coalition government composed of two or more parties. When potential voters believe that elections are not important, they tend to refrain from voting (Franklin 1996; Jackman 1987); thus turnout tends to be lower in multiparty systems. The higher turnout rate in PR systems is the result, as noted above, of fewer wasted votes, since citizens know that as long as their party meets a minimum threshold they will receive representation in government. The plurality system in the United States simultaneously constrains turnout because of wasted votes and fosters turnout (at least minimally) because of the reduced number of parties.

The body of research on proportional versus plurality electoral systems indicates that turnout is higher in PR systems than in plurality systems. Given the unique institutional features of the United States, however, it is difficult to empirically pinpoint the absence of a PR system as a substantial reason for the lower turnout rate in American elections. However, as Powell (1986) argued, single-member district systems, such as the one used in the United States, have an impact on the competitive context of national elections and thus have an impact on national-level turnout. For example, in nations that choose the executive by a simple national plurality or majority (what we would call the popular vote in American presidential elections) and in proportional systems with national districts or large multimember districts, parties have incentive to mobilize the entire nation. As a result of the national mobilization efforts, turnout tends to be even across the nation. In effect, all citizens are potentially mobilized by the parties in an election. Although some districts in SMD systems are very competitive and the parties expend great effort to mobilize their supporters and potential supporters to win contested elections, other districts are very uncompetitive. The parties have little incentive to mobilize the electorate in these districts because the outcome is relatively certain. As a result, party mobilization efforts will be uneven in SMD systems when compared to systems with nationally competitive districts, and turnout should therefore be lower (see also Jackman 1987; Jackman and Miller 1995).

Figure 4.2 presents mean turnout rates in our sample of countries across the different levels of district competitiveness.[5] The nations with the smallest districts (or the most local) have the lowest levels of turnout. Between 1960 and 2000, countries with SMD elections had a mean turnout rate of 72.15 percent and nations with districts of three to five members had a mean turnout rate of 71.61 percent. The two categories of nations with large districts have higher rates than the two local categories. Countries with large multimember districts have a mean turnout rate of 77.22 percent. Powell hypothesized that nations with national districts or national plurality/majority elections would have the highest turnout rate of 81.38 percent. The data presented in Figure 4.2 suggest that electoral systems based on nationally competitive districts do have higher levels of turnout than systems based on relatively small and local districts.

In terms of nationally competitive districts, the United States is classified in the least competitive category. Senate elections are

FIG 4.2   Turnout Comparison Across District Size, 1960–2000

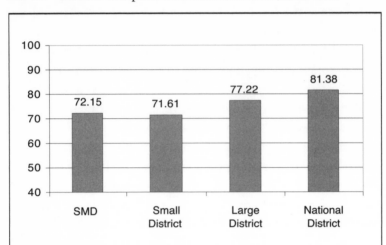

Source: International Institute for Electoral Assistance;
Federal Elections Commission

winner-take-all, with each state holding separate plurality elections for each Senate seat. The House of Representatives holds pure SMD elections for its 435 seats, and the president is elected through the uniquely American Electoral College. It is based on a bloc vote determined by plurality rules, and each state is treated as an individual district (with the exception of Maine and Nebraska). Some congressional districts and states are very competitive with election outcomes uncertain until the election, while in other states and districts the outcome of the election is all but predetermined. Because competitiveness varies across electoral districts (states included), there should be great variation in the degree to which the parties and candidates seek to mobilize potential supporters, instead of the relatively even mobilization efforts across nations with national competitive electoral districts (e.g., France's simple majority for president or the national PR districts used in Israel and the Netherlands). Because mobilization efforts are uneven across the United States, turnout should be lower in the noncompetitive districts and higher in competitive districts. When compared to systems with more nationally competitive districts, then, turnout in U.S. national elections should be lower.

The goal of this chapter was to place the United States and its plurality electoral system in the broader context of electoral systems across industrialized democracies. Clearly the plurality system has an effect on national turnout rates. The analysis in the next two chapters will examine closely the impact of SMD on national turnout rates in the United States. Using Powell's logic about the impact of SMD elections on the competitive context of national elections, Chapter 5 will examine the effect that the Electoral College has on turnout in presidential elections, and Chapter 6 will focus on the turnout in House of Representatives elections.

Notes

1. The most notable example of the corrective system is the one used in Germany. The national legislature (the Bundestag) has 656 seats; 328 of them are elected through single-member districts. The remaining 328 seats are chosen in a national election and allocated based on PR rules. The method of allocation compensates parties that did not fare well in the SMD elections and thus produces a more proportional allocation of seats, even if it means adding seats to the Bundestag (Blais and Massicotte 1996; Powell 2000; Shick and Zeh 1999).

2. See Appendix A for the list of countries used in this analysis, including each country's type of electoral system and its average turnout rate between 1960 and 2000. Australia, Belgium, and Italy have compulsory voting laws mandating that all citizens participate in elections. While compulsory voting laws are associated with higher levels of turnout, these countries are included in this analysis because their exclusion would not substantively alter the results. Italy's law enforcement is considered weak and consequently the laws likely have little effect on turnout. While Belgium and Australia strictly enforce their compulsory voting laws, Belgium is a PR state in this analysis and Australia is a plurality state; thus they tend to neutralize each other in the comparison between PR and plurality systems.

3. PR systems vary, with some systems exhibiting a greater degree of proportionality. When the impact of electoral systems on turnout is examined,

however, the difference in turnout tends to be between PR systems and plurality systems (Blais 2000). Because of this, list systems, single-transferable vote systems, and mixed corrective systems are classified as PR systems.

4. The data used in Figure 4.1 include both Switzerland and the United States in the group of countries classified as majoritarian systems. Both countries have unique institutional features that have an impact on turnout and therefore are generally excluded from analyses examining electoral systems and turnout or at least controlled for in multivariate models (see Jackman 1987; Powell 1982, 1986 on the institutional features of Switzerland). The data presented in this chapter are for illustration purposes, and the patterns evident in the figures are consistent with studies that controlled for Switzerland and the United States (Jackman 1987; Jackman and Miller 1995; Powell 1986).

5. The classification used here is taken from Powell (1986). The countries are coded as follows: single-member district or winner-take-all; small multi-member PR (3–5 members); large multimember PR; simple national vote for presidency or national PR. See Appendix A for each country's classification.

5

Winner-Take-All Elections, Part I

The Electoral College: Strategy, Mobilization, and Turnout

In Chapter 4 we examined the impact of various electoral systems on turnout. In this chapter we will focus on the unique electoral mechanism the United States uses to select the president: the Electoral College (EC).[1] The process of selecting the president through the Electoral College is fairly straightforward. Each state is allocated a number of electoral votes equal to its total congressional delegation: the total number of representatives plus two senators.[2] For example, the state of Georgia has thirteen members in the U.S. House of Representatives and two senators, and thus it has fifteen electoral votes. The total number of electoral votes for all states and the District of Columbia is 538; to win the presidency a candidate must win a majority, or 270 electoral votes.[3]

The process of selecting the president takes place in the following manner. On Election Day, all states and the District of Columbia hold elections. On the Monday following the second Wednesday in December, electors meet in their respective state capitals and cast one vote for president and one vote for vice president.[4] The Constitution does not mandate that state electors vote to reflect the outcome of the popular election in their state; indeed, elector independence from the popular will was one purpose of the Electoral College. However, the modern Electoral College encourages electors to cast their votes to reflect the outcome of the election. For instance, prior to the election the parties (and in some cases independent candidates) provide to the head election official in the state (usually the secretary of state) a list of individuals pledged to the party's candidate (electors). The party whose candidate wins the popular vote sends its electors to the state capitol, and they naturally cast their vote for the party's candidate (Federal Elections Commission).[5]

The Constitution left the manner in which electors are chosen to the states. Consequently states experimented with various methods of selecting electors, and two methods emerged: appointment by the state legislature or election by popular vote.[6] By 1832 only South Carolina did not use popular selection for electors.[7] The predominate method for popular election was an at-large system that awarded all of a state's electors to the winner of the state's popular vote (Dahl 2002); today forty-eight states and the District of Columbia use this system.[8]

The EC was not necessarily based on sound theoretical foundations. Rather, it was the final choice among several proposed options considered during the last week of the Constitutional Convention (Dahl 2002). While the framers struggled with the precise mechanism for choosing the president, they largely agreed that a layer of decisionmaking was needed between the citizenry and the election of the president. Many delegates believed that selecting the president through a popular election would produce less than ideal individuals to take the office (Lutz, Abbott, Allen, and Hansen 2002). Given that the EC removes the selection of the president from the electorate and places it in the hands of electors who cast a state's electoral votes for a candidate, it is an inherently undemocratic institution (Dahl 2002). For example, as the 2000 presidential election demonstrated, the winner of the popular vote (the candidate with the most votes) can indeed lose the election.[9] In fact, on three other occasions since the ratification of the Constitution, the winner of the popular vote did not win the majority of electoral votes and thus did not win the presidency.[10] The Electoral College also creates an unequal representation of voters. Because each state is given two electoral votes for its two senators (plus the number of House of Representatives members), small states have a disproportionately larger share of representation in the Electoral College. For example, in the ten smallest states the number of citizens per elector ranges from 165,000 to 300,000, while in the ten largest states the range is 586,000 to 628,000 citizens per elector. This disproportionality in representation gives small states a greater share of power in choosing the president than they would have if the number of electors was based on population alone, and therefore it serves as a barrier to majority rule (Dahl 2002).

The winner-take-all nature of the Electoral College also creates disadvantages. First, winner-take-all elections create disincentives for minor party candidates to effectively compete, and thus the EC system helps facilitate the dominance of the two-party system in the United States (Bibby 2003; Dahl 2002). Second, in states that are not competitive, many voters (particularly supporters of the disadvantaged party) may choose to abstain because they see no point in participating in an election when their candidate is guaranteed to lose (Dahl 2002). Finally, given that some states are competitive and some uncompetitive, the presidential campaigns have little incentive to expend campaign resources in states where the outcome is certain; instead, they allocate the bulk of their resources to a small group of competitive or battleground states (Dahl 2002; Hill and Mckee 2005; Mayer, Buell, Campbell, and Joslyn 2002; Shaw 1999). The remainder of this chapter will focus on the impact of Electoral College campaign strategy on turnout.

The Electoral College and Campaign Strategy

As the central governing institution of presidential elections, the Electoral College constrains and shapes the behavior of the candidates in the election in two ways. First, in order to win the presidency a candidate must win a minimum of 270 electoral votes. Second, in order to achieve the 270 vote threshold candidates must win elections in individual states. Taken together, these requirements force presidential campaigns to develop strategies based on winning enough states to achieve the minimum 270 electoral vote threshold (Brams and Davis 1974; Colantoni, Levesque, and Ordeshook 1975; Bartels 1985; James and Lawson 1999; Shaw 1999).

In developing Electoral College strategies, the campaigns are determining which states should receive their limited resources, both instrumental and ornamental. Instrumental resources are assets used to win votes. Bartels (1985) argues that in presidential campaigns media advertising and candidate visits to states are instrumental resources—direct efforts at winning votes. Ornamental resources, on the other hand, "satisfy the internal and public relations needs of the campaign organization" (Bartels 1985, 932). In terms of strategies developed to win a majority in the Electoral College, the allocation of instrumental resources is the key decision facing the campaign.[11]

One perspective on Electoral College strategies is that candidates seek to win states with the most electoral votes and thus allocate most of their resources to these states (Brams and Davis 1974; Bartels 1985). On its face, this strategy seems justified. For example, in the 2000 presidential election the eight largest states (CA, FL, IL, MI, NY, OH, PA, TX) had a total of 225 electoral votes, 83 percent of the electoral votes needed to win the presidency. From this perspective, we would expect presidential campaigns to mainly compete in this small group of states.

Campaign resources are finite, however, and therefore campaigns must allocate their funds in a way that maximizes their effectiveness in reaching the goal of 270 EC votes (James and Lawson 1999; Shaw 1999). Because not all states are competitive, campaigns have no incentive to expend resources where they are assured of either victory or defeat (Texas and New York, the second and third largest states, are two examples of this in 2000 and 2004). Instead, the campaigns have great incentive to focus resources on states in which the outcome is uncertain or doubtful—battleground or swing states. This is where the campaigns in a presidential election choose to wage their battle for the presidency (James and Lawson 1999; Shaw 1999). Thus in most presidential elections we would expect to see the majority of resources expended in states where the outcome is relatively uncertain as both campaigns attempt to reach 270 EC votes.

Campaigns tend to place states in one of five categories: base Democrat, base Republican, marginal Democrat, marginal Republican, and battleground.[12] *Base states,* the least competitive, are a certain lock for the respective party in the upcoming election. *Marginal states,* while leaning toward one party, are competitive enough to warrant attention from the campaigns. *Battleground states,* where the outcome of the campaign is undetermined prior to the campaign, receive most of the campaigns' resources.

In categorizing a state, campaigns focus on its electoral competitiveness, the number of electoral votes available, and the cost of TV advertising. This is not to say that competitive states, those with large numbers of electoral votes, or those with cheap advertising will be classified as battleground states. Instead, states that have a large number of electoral votes *and* are competitive are likely to be classified as battleground states. Those that have inexpensive advertising available *and* are competitive are also likely to be classified as battleground states. Thus competitiveness appears to be the central factor in determining whether or not a campaign classifies a state as a battleground state, although the effect is conditioned by the size of the state and the cost of advertising (Shaw 1999).

In terms of resource allocation, Shaw (1999) found that between 1988 and 1996 the battleground states received the most media spending and candidate visits from the campaigns, while the marginal states received noticeably less. The base states (or those least competitive) received by far the smallest allocation of resources.

Figure 5.1 presents the distribution of media spending based on state classification between 1988 and 2000. The more important a state was to the outcome of the election, the more media spending it received from the campaigns. Base states received the smallest amount

FIG 5.1   Media Spending by Battleground Status, 1988–2000
(Total GRPs Purchased)

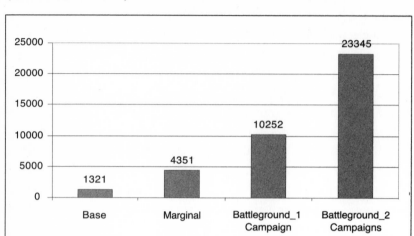

between 1998 and 2000 (mean of 1,321 GRPs).[13] Marginal states received three times more GRPs (4,351) than the base states, although
much less than the two groups of battlegrounds. The states considered
battlegrounds by only one campaign received an average of 10,252
GRPs, while those considered battlegrounds by both campaigns received a mean of 23,345 GRPs. Clearly the campaigns devoted the bulk
of their resources to a relatively small group of states.[14]

Figure 5.2 presents the mean number of candidate visits across the
four classifications of battleground status. As with media spending,
the more important a state was considered to the outcome of the
Electoral College competition, the more candidate visits it received.
For example, base and marginal states received an average of four
and six visits respectively by either a major party presidential candidate or vice presidential candidate. Battleground states (1 and 2 campaign), on the other hand, received an average nine and ten
candidate visits. Clearly the more important a state was considered
in determining the outcome of the election, the more likely presidential and vice presidential candidates were to visit. Interestingly, the

FIG 5.2   Candidate Visits by Battleground Status, 1988–2000

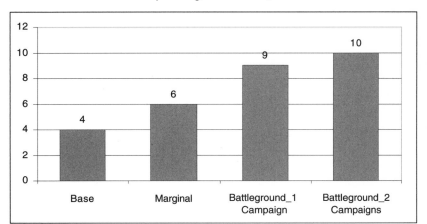

difference in visits between the two groups of battleground states and the base and marginal states is not as great as it is with media spending.[15]

Of course, the funds and visits expended by presidential campaigns at the state level could also be the result of other factors. For example, a highly competitive gubernatorial, senatorial, or House race might induce the parties as well as the candidates' organizations to spend money or even visit the state to influence the outcome of an important gubernatorial or congressional race. Consequently, it is necessary to examine resource allocation with the use of multivariate regression in order to estimate the impact of battleground status on spending and visits while taking into account other factors such as gubernatorial or senatorial race, the percentage of House races that are competitive, and the state's number of electoral votes. Table 5.1 presents the least squares dummy variables estimates of resource allocation in presidential elections from 1988 to 2000.[16] The results presented in Table 5.1 are consistent with previous research on resource allocation in presidential elections (Shaw 1999; Hill and Mckee 2005). The only coefficient to have a significant impact on media spending is the battleground status variable. The coefficient for battleground status

TABLE 5.1   LSDV Estimates of Resource Allocation in Presidential
Campaigns, 1988–2000

	Media Spending (GRPs)	Candidate Visits
Gubernatorial race	94.74	−25
	(1133.69)	(1.44)
Senatorial race	−655.69	1.47
	(935.30)	(1.19)
Competitive house races (%)	−9.02	0.004
	(19.81)	(0.025)
Electoral votes	61.65	0.166
	(108.91)	(0.138)
Battleground status	6546.59**	−.419
	(693.63)	(.883)
Battleground * Electoral votes	−67.41	.107*
	(45.57)	(.058)
Constant	−4871.02	1.72
	(1631.73)	(2.07)
n	200	200
Adjusted R^2	.46	.19

NOTE: Standard errors are in parentheses.
* $p < .05$, **$p<.01$ one-tailed test

suggests that every one-unit increase in the ordinal classification of
battleground states (e.g., moving from a base state to a marginal state)
resulted in a roughly 6,500 GRP increase. The difference in allocated
GRPs between a base state and state considered a battleground state by
both campaigns is 19,638.[17]

The second column in Table 5.1 presents the LSDV estimates for
candidate visits. The only coefficient to have a significant impact on
the number of candidate visits is the interaction term for electoral
votes and battleground states. The coefficient for the interaction term
indicates that every one-electoral vote increase *and* a one-unit increase in the ordinal classification resulted in an increase of about
one-tenth of a visit. The findings presented in Table 5.1 are consistent
with what Hill and Mckee (2005) found concerning the 2000 presi-

dential election: the number of electoral votes has no impact on media spending, but electoral votes do condition the impact of battleground status on candidate visits. In terms of candidate visits, the campaigns used their most valuable resource—the candidates—where they would receive the greatest return: battleground states with a large number of electoral votes.

In their efforts to build an Electoral College strategy, the presidential campaigns devoted the bulk of their finite campaign resources to states where the election outcome was relatively uncertain. The remainder of this chapter will focus on the relationship between battleground status, campaign resource allocation, and turnout.

Campaigns and Turnout

In presidential elections, the major campaigns develop strategies about how to allocate relatively scarce resources to win an electoral vote majority. As already noted, those resources are not allocated evenly across all states. The battleground states receive the most resources; the marginal states receive less than the battleground states but more than the uncompetitive base states. As noted in the previous chapter, nations with single-member district electoral systems tend to have lower turnout rates than nations with systems that elect either the executive or the parliament in national districts or large multimember districts. This pattern exists because in single-member district systems some districts will be uncompetitive and receive little attention from the campaigns while others will be very competitive and receive a great deal of attention. Consequently because of the increased resource allocation by the campaigns in the battleground states (and to an extent the marginal states), turnout should be higher than in the base states.

A central debate in the study of electoral participation is whether or not close elections stimulate turnout. A controversial perspective is that close elections create an environment in which citizens perceive their vote will be decisive (or at least important) in determining the outcome of the election and consequently are more likely to overcome the costs associated with voting (Blais 2001; Downs 1956; Riker and Ordeshook 1968). In close elections, then, more citizens perceive that their vote will make a difference in the outcome of the election, and thus more citizens turn out on Election Day to cast a ballot.

Critics of this argument contend that even in very close elections there is almost no likelihood that an individual citizen's vote will be decisive, and thus it is unlikely that individuals vote because they believe their vote will be decisive.[18] While this critique is valid, in their study of U.S. House races Cox and Munger (1989) found that even when controlling for demographics, statewide races, and campaign expenditures, the closeness of House races was positively related to turnout. The authors rightly conclude that some citizens appeared to be casting ballots due the uncertainty of the outcome of House races. In a local election such as a House race, the relatively small size of the electorate may increase the perceived importance of a citizen's vote on the outcome and thus increase turnout. In the national presidential election, however, closeness should have less of an effect because the size of the electorate should reduce a citizen's perceived impact. Even at the state level the closeness of the presidential race within a state should have less effect because of the size of the electorate.

The evidence concerning whether or not close elections induce citizens to vote instrumentally is inconclusive; it is likely that in the context of close elections, the parties, candidates, and supporters increase their efforts to maximize their chances of winning (Cox and Munger 1989; Rosenstone and Hansen 1993; Jackson 1997). As noted, in his examination of Electoral College strategies Shaw (1999) found that campaigns tended to allocate greater resources to marginal and battleground states than in relatively sure battleground states, and the data in the previous section seem to verify this pattern (see also Hill and McKee 2005). Apparently the uncertainty and greater stakes of close elections cause candidates (and allies) to devote greater resources to mobilization efforts (Rosenstone and Hansen 1993).

Mobilization efforts can take place through a variety of methods. The campaigns, for instance, can directly contact citizens through the mail, over the phone, or by face-to-face canvassing (Gerber and Green 2000;

Gerber and Green 2001). While phone calls and mail contact have little to no effect on turnout (Gerber and Green 2000; Gerber and Green 2001), face-to-face contact has been significantly and positively related to turnout (Wielhouwer and Lockerbie 1994; Wielhouwer 2000; Gerber and Green 2000). Another method of direct campaigning is the traditional campaign rally, in which the candidate appears before a crowd of supporters. In a national election this type of retail campaigning is not likely to have a substantial impact on the overall outcome. However, at the local level a visit by a presidential candidate can have a modest positive effect on turnout. Jones (1998) found that in a presidential election a visit by a candidate of either of the two major parties to a media market increased turnout by about half a percentage point in that market. Furthermore, this effect is cumulative, so in a highly competitive state in which candidates are likely to visit a large media market many times there should be a noticeable effect on turnout at the local level.

In most large-scale elections, particularly the national presidential election, the bulk of campaign resources (i.e., money) is devoted to television advertising, which can reach larger numbers of potential voters than face-to-face or other forms of direct contact. The effect of television advertising on turnout is subject to debate, however, largely centering on whether negative advertising depresses turnout, stimulates turnout, or has no effect. Early work on the topic found that exposure to negative campaign ads reduced the likelihood that an individual would cast a ballot in an upcoming election (Ansolabehere and Iyengar, 1995; Ansolabehere, Iyengar, and Simon 1999; Ansolabehere, Iyengar, Simon, and Valentine 1994). Recently several researchers have found that rather than having a depressive effect on turnout, negative advertising appears to stimulate turnout or at least has no significant effect (Finkel and Geer 1998; Freedman and Goldstein 1999; Fridkin Kahn, and Kenney 1999; Wattenberg and Brians 1999; Goldstein and Freedman 2002).[19] Although this debate has not been conclusively resolved, it is reasonable to think that increased advertising results in greater campaign visibility. The greater visibility of the campaign should produce more interest in the campaign among the electorate, and turnout should subsequently increase (Bullock, Gaddie, and Ferrington 2002).

Rosenstone and Hansen (1993, 2001) argue that mobilization increases turnout, in large part, because as candidates and parties seek electoral support to increase their chances of winning elections, they reduce the costs of participation for potential voters (see also Aldrich 1993). When candidates and/or parties directly contact potential voters, whether through the mail, over the phone, or by face-to-face canvassing, they inform potential voters about when, where, and how they can vote; they notify them of upcoming rallies and visits by the candidates, and even provide transportation for those who need it on Election Day (Rosenstone and Hansen 1993). Given the reduced costs, it is not surprising that direct contact by parties and candidates is significantly and positively related to turnout (Wielhouwer and Lockerbie 1994; Wielhouwer 2001; Gerber and Green 2000). Media advertising and candidate visits create an information-rich environment, reducing the costs of acquiring campaign information for the average citizen.

Figures 5.1 and 5.2 show that the more competitive the campaigns deemed a state, the more media spending and candidate visits the state received. Given the relationship between mobilization and turnout noted above, higher levels of spending and visits received by battleground states should also result in higher levels of turnout (Hill and Mckee 2005). Table 5.2 presents the LSDV estimates for state-level turnout in presidential elections between 1988 and 2000. If the argument that greater levels of spending and candidate visits result in higher levels of turnout is correct, the coefficients for spending and visits should be significant while controlling for other state-level contextual and political factors. While the coefficient for candidate visits is not significantly related to state-level turnout, media spending is significantly and positively related to turnout, indicating that increased media spending by the campaigns results in increases in state-level turnout. For example, a one standard deviation unit increase in media spending (9685.45 GRPs) increases turnout by approximately three-quarters of a percentage point.

As with the Shaw and Hill and McKee projects, the analysis presented in this chapter thus far suggests that (1) the major campaigns in presidential elections devote the bulk of the campaign resources to the

TABLE 5.2   LSDV Estimates of State-Level Turnout, 1988–2000

	Unstandardized Coefficients	Standard Errors
Registered (%)	.251**	.63
College degree (%)	.373**	.09
Per capita income	.03**	.01
South	−3.41	.797
Closing date	−.218**	.04
Racial diversity	−.177**	.03
Gubernatorial race	−.849	1.05
Senate race	−380	.69
Gubernatorial race X gubernatorial spending	−.0001	.0001
Senate race X senate spending	.00002	.00003
Battleground status	.128	.39
Candidate visits	.035	.03
Media spending	.0008*	.00004
Constant	44.34**	2.80
n	200	
Adjusted R^2	.62	

NOTE: Standard errors are in parentheses.
* p < .05, **p<.01 one-tailed test

states they deem the most important to the outcome of the Electoral College contest—the battleground states—and (2) increases in spending by the major campaigns resulted in modest levels of state-level turnout. Taken together, these analyses suggest that the higher levels of spending in battleground states should result in higher levels of turnout in these states, and thus there is an indirect relationship between battleground status and turnout. Figure 5.3 illustrates how this indirect relationship between battleground status and turnout works. The more important a state is deemed in determining the outcome of the electoral college vote, the more media spending it receives. Greater media spending then results in greater turnout. To calculate the exact

FIG 5.3   Indirect Effects of Battleground Status on Turnout

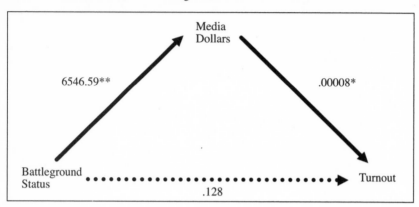

indirect effect, we multiply the battleground status coefficient from the media spending model in Table 5.1 (6546.59) times the media spending coefficient in the turnout model in Table 5.2 (.00008), for an indirect effect of half a percentage point (.52) for every one unit increase in the ordinal classification. Therefore, the turnout difference between battleground states recognized by both campaigns and base states due to the effects of media spending is 1.57 percentage points.

As noted earlier, Hill and Mckee (2005) found that if the Bush and Gore campaigns would have allocated to all states the spending that went to the battleground states, national turnout would have increased by three to five percentage points. Figure 5.4 presents the predicted national turnout based on various levels of spending.[20] The baseline predicted turnout is 56 percent (which is one percentage point lower than actual mean turnout in the elections considered here). If all states from 1988 to 2000 would have received the mean level of spending (23,345 GRPs) for the states considered battlegrounds by both major campaigns, national turnout would have been 57 percent, or a one-percentage point increase. If spending in all states would have matched the level of one standard deviation unit above the mean (38,278 GRPs), national turnout would have been 58 percent, and if all states would have received the maximum level of spending in the battle-

FIG 5.4   Predicted National Turnout Based on Battleground State Media Spending, 1988–2000

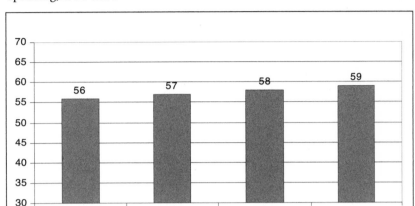

ground states (45,763), turnout would have increased by three percentage points to 59 percent. Apparently the uneven mobilization created by the EC constrains turnout to a lower level than it could be if all states were treated equally.

The Electoral College and Increased Citizen Involvement

The argument that increased mobilization efforts in battleground states lead to higher turnout is based on the assumption that the campaigns' efforts to win votes increases the involvement of citizens in these states and that increased involvement, in turn, leads to a higher probability that citizens will vote in an election. While involvement in politics is generally measured by a number of variables (interest in the campaign, political efficacy, a sense of civic duty, partisanship), it essentially indicates the degree to which a citizen is engaged with the political world and/or current election. The body of research on electoral participation establishes that the more engaged a citizen is with the political world, the greater her likelihood of voting in elections (see Conway 2000). Therefore, if mobilization increases citizen involvement during the course of a campaign, it is reasonable to expect turnout to increase.

In his book *The Vanishing Voter* Thomas Patterson demonstrates this point in the context of the 2000 presidential political election.[21] He argues that in highly competitive elections such as 2000, the increased campaign activity in the battleground states results in greater citizen involvement. Patterson defines involvement by whether or not a citizen thought about the campaign daily, recalled a campaign news story daily, talked about the campaign daily, or voted in the past election. Consistent with the analyses presented in this chapter, Patterson found that citizens in battleground states were more likely to be contacted by the campaigns than citizens in nonbattleground states. For example, 57 percent of citizens living in battleground states received campaign mail, compared to 46 percent of citizens residing in nonbattleground states. Forty-seven percent of citizens in battleground states received a phone call related to the campaign, compared to 31 percent of citizens in nonbattleground states; 9 percent of battleground state citizens received a visit from a campaign worker compared to 7 percent of citizens in nonbattleground states. Clearly residents of battleground states were more likely to be contacted by the campaigns.

Patterson also found that citizens in battleground states were more involved in the campaign than citizens in nonbattleground states. For example, 58 percent of citizens in battleground states stated that they thought about the campaign daily, while only 43 percent of citizens living in nonbattleground states stated this. Forty-seven percent of battleground state citizens stated that they recalled a campaign news story daily, compared to 42 percent in nonbattleground states. Forty-seven percent of citizens in battleground states stated that they talked about the campaign daily, while only 43 percent of nonbattleground state citizens said they did. Finally, 55 percent of battleground state citizens stated that they voted, versus only 50 percent of nonbattleground state citizens. Patterson's work suggests that citizens in battleground states are more likely to be contacted by the campaigns and as a result are noticeably more engaged than citizens in nonbattleground states.

Solutions

The evidence presented in this chapter, as well as the work of other authors, clearly suggests that the Electoral College skews the allocation of resources in presidential elections toward a handful of competitive states, increasing turnout modestly in these states, while the rest of the nation is relatively ignored. This uneven mobilization reduces turnout to a lower level than it could be if resources were allocated equally across all states. The question is, What would happen if the Electoral College were eliminated or substantially modified? Abolishing the EC would be very difficult. First, as noted in Chapter 3, the Constitution is difficult to amend. The requirement of a two-thirds vote in both houses and ratification by three-quarters of the states (38) makes any substantial change to the Constitution unlikely. Second, given that small states are somewhat advantaged in the EC, they are unlikely to acquiesce to changes that would dramatically alter their status in the selection of the president. Thus small states are likely to use the difficulty of the amending process to prevent any change. For instance, around seven hundred proposals have been introduced to alter or abolish the EC, and none was ever passed by both houses of Congress. In 1989 the House of Representatives, reflecting broad support in the electorate, passed a bill providing for the popular election of the president by a vote of 338–70 (or 83 percent of the vote). This bill was then filibustered in the Senate. Proponents of the bill gained the support of only fifty-four senators (54 percent), well short of the sixty votes needed to end a filibuster and the sixty-seven votes needed to achieve the required two-thirds vote (Dahl 2002). Even if the bill had made it out of the Senate and been signed by the president, it is unlikely that thirty-eight states would have ratified it. The other two alternatives, proportional allocation of electoral votes and the district system (each of which will be discussed below), would be much easier to achieve because the manner of EC vote allocation is determined by each state and thus would not require a constitutional amendment.

Elimination of the EC would lead to increased turnout because the campaigns would have to allocate the resources equally across the nation. Critics counter that under a popular vote system the campaigns would simply target the largest media markets and ignore the remainder of the nation (Dahl 2002; Mayer, Buell, Campbell, and Joslyn 2002; Stein, Johnson, Shaw, and Weissberg 2002). Under the popular vote system the campaigns would most likely target population centers. However, the demographic heterogeneity of cities virtually guarantees that a campaign could not lock up a popular vote plurality or majority by focusing solely on a limited set of population centers (Mayer, Buell, Campbell, and Joslyn 2002). Under a popular vote system, and absent the zero-sum proposition under the EC, we would likely see candidates compete for votes in many more states because now there would be a greater payoff in capturing a larger share of the vote in states candidates cannot carry (e.g., Bush in New York and Kerry in Texas). As Dahl notes, in close popular vote elections the campaigns will seek out votes "wherever they might be available" (Dahl 2002, 85).

Given the difficulty of amending the Constitution, we are stuck with the Electoral College and change must come at the state level. There are two potential state-level reforms that could occur. The first is proportional allocation of electoral votes. Under this system the electoral votes would be distributed to candidates based on their share of the popular vote. As with the popular vote, in close elections, the proportional allocation of electoral votes would create incentive for the campaigns to seek electoral votes in states that might lose (Mayer, Buell, Campbell, and Josyln 2002). For example, gaining only 40 percent of the popular vote in a proportional system means gaining 40 percent of the electoral vote, a different decision calculus for the campaigns than a context in which 40 percent of the popular vote means no electoral votes. Because of this, more money would likely be expended in marginal states and even base states. Given that turnout is related to expenditures, turnout would likely increase at least modestly under this system.

The final alternative is the district system currently used in Nebraska and Maine. The winner of the overall state vote is awarded two electoral votes and the winner of each congressional district is awarded one electoral vote. While the campaigns in this system are likely to contest competitive districts in uncompetitive states, the bias will be much like the current system in that the campaigns would focus much of their resources on competitive congressional districts while ignoring uncompetitive districts (Mayer, Buell, Campbell, and Joslyn 2002; Stein, Johnson, Shaw, and Weissberg 2002). If this is the case, then it is unlikely turnout would increase. Stein, Johnson, Shaw, and Weissberg (2002) note that because congressional districts and media markets do not always overlap, the use of the modern media campaign under a district system would be difficult, and as a result the campaigns may be forced to turn to more grassroots oriented, direct mobilization efforts. It is possible that turnout would increase "nontrivially," given the strong relationship between direct mobilization and turnout. As the authors note, however, because the parties target their efforts toward particular groups, the district system is unlikely to produce dramatic changes in turnout.

The research on the Electoral College and the data presented in this chapter demonstrate that because the Electoral College system is composed of what are effectively forty-nine winner-take-all single-member districts, the variation of competitiveness across states structures the campaign efforts of the two parties in a way that skews the bulk of available campaign resources toward the small group of battleground states. As a result turnout is higher in these states than in the rest of the nation. Because this group of states is normally small, national turnout is lower than it could be if all states were treated equally. In the next chapter we will examine the impact of varying competitiveness across House of Representatives districts and its impact on turnout.

Notes

1. The data for this chapter were provided by Daron Shaw at the University of Texas. Opinions, findings, conclusions, or recommendations expressed are

those of the author. Much of the analysis presented in this chapter is adapted from Hill and Mckee (2005).

2. Although the District of Columbia has no congressional delegation, it is awarded three electoral votes, since this is the minimum number of electoral votes a state can have (the minimum number of House members is one and each state has two senators).

3. If no candidate wins a majority of electoral votes, the election is turned over to the House of Representatives. Within the House each state delegation casts one vote for its preferred candidate. The winner of the majority of the fifty votes cast in the House is elected president.

4. The Constitution originally gave each elector two votes for president. In the election of 1800 each elector who cast a ballot for Jefferson also cast a ballot for his prospective vice president, Aaron Burr, and the election ended in a tie between Jefferson and Burr. After thirty-six ballots in the House of Representatives, Jefferson was elected president. As a result the Twelfth Amendment, which provided each elector one vote for president and one vote for vice president, was ratified in 1804.

5. Since 1796, 156 "faithless electors" have cast ballots for someone other than their party's designated candidate. Only eight of these "faithless electors" cast ballots in the twentieth century, the most recent in 2000. The actions of faithless electors have never affected the outcome of the election. Seventeen states have laws that forbid electors from casting a ballot different from the outcome of the popular vote.

6. William C. Kimberling, *The Electoral College,* report produced by the Federal Elections Commission, www.fec.gov/pdf/eleccoll.pdf.

7. Electors in South Carolina were chosen by the state legislature, but this was abandoned in favor of popular election following the Civil War (Dahl 2002).

8. Some states chose a district vote in which the winner of the popular vote in each congressional district is awarded one electoral vote and the winner of the overall state popular vote is awarded two electoral votes (one per senator). Maine and Nebraska are the only states that currently use this system. All other states use the at-large winner-take-all system.

9. Al Gore won the popular vote by a margin of 543,895 votes (one-half of one percentage point), but George W. Bush won the EC with a bare majority of 271 electoral votes and was therefore awarded the presidency (Federal Elections Commission).

10. In 1824 Andrew Jackson won a plurality of the popular vote and a plurality of the Electoral College vote, but the House of Representatives chose

John Quincy Adams to be president. In 1876 Samuel Tilden won the popular vote but lost the Electoral College vote to Rutherford B. Hayes, and in 1888 Grover Cleveland won a majority of the popular vote but lost the Electoral College vote to Benjamin Harrison (Lutz, Abbott, Allen, and Hanson 2002).

11. For the remainder of the chapter I will use "resources" in lieu of "instrumental resources."

12. Shaw (2004) argues that the extreme closeness of the 2000 election led the two campaigns to narrow the field of contested states to a relatively small group of battleground states and allocate the bulk of their resources to these states rather than using the traditional ordinal classification.

13. The total number of gross ratings points (GRPs) is an approximation of audience exposure to campaign advertisements. One hundred GRPs are roughly equal to the average viewer seeing an ad once. Put another way, total GRPs purchased in a state media market (i.e., Boston) indicate approximately how many times the typical viewer will see an advertisement in that specific market. GRPs are useful in the analysis of media spending because they equalize market advertising cost discrepancies. This is important given that the cost of advertising in New York City, for instance, is higher than in Omaha, Nebraska; and without some sort of adjustment comparisons would be difficult if not impossible. For each state the media spending variable is constructed by dividing the total advertising dollars spent (Gore/DNC + Bush/RNC) in each media market by the average cost per 100 GRPs in that market, then multiplying this quotient by the percentage of the state's registered voters in that market. This procedure is repeated for all of a state's markets (where advertising was purchased), and the resulting products from each market are summed to get the final statewide value. More formally, the media spending calculation is:

$$\text{Media Spending} = \sum \frac{(Total\$_i)}{(Cost_i)} * (Market\ Share_i)$$

The calculations of GRPs purchased are taken from Shaw (1999); see also Hill and McKee (2005).

14. Two hundred states were considered in the analysis (50 states for 4 elections). Of the two hundred states in the analysis only fifty-six were either states considered battleground states by one campaign (33) or states considered battleground states by both campaigns (23).

15. Hill and Mckee (2005) found that while candidate visits were related to battleground status (although not as strong as media spending), it was conditioned by the number of electoral votes; battleground states that had a large

number of electoral votes tended to receive the most candidate visits. The effect was not evident for media spending.

16. This chapter relies on pooled–cross-sectional data (states and years are the units of analysis). Because the dataset is dominated by cross-sections (50 states and only 4 elections), the analysis uses least squares dummy variables (LSDV) or fixed effects models. The latter include the independent variables of interest and a dummy variable for each unit (years in this analysis) to correct for possible heteroskedasticity and autocorrelation resulting from some underlying, yet unmeasured influence across units (Hsiao 1986; Stimson 1985).

17. The figure was arrived at by multiplying the coefficient in the spending model (6546.59) by three, or the three-unit move up the ordinal classification.

18. A sizable minority of citizens likely overestimate the importance of their vote in determining the outcome of the election and thus vote instrumentally, although their vote did not actually play an important role in determining the outcome of the election.

19. See Lau, Sigelman, Heldman, and Babbit (1999) for an impressive meta-analysis of the research on the effects of negative advertising.

20. This estimate is calculated as expected turnout $_{2000}$ = 44.34+ (registered percent * .251) + (college percent * .373) + (per capita income * .03) + (South * –3.41) + (closing date * –.218) + (racial diversity * –.177) + (gubernatorial race * –.849) + (Senate race * –.380) + (gubernatorial race X log of gubernatorial expenditures * –.0001) + (Senate race X log of senatorial expenditures * .00002) + (battleground status * –.128) + (candidate visits * .035) + (Total GRPs * .0008). To calculate the base national turnout, the above model multiplied each state's actual level of media spending and candidate visits by the respective coefficients for media spending and candidate visits. To calculate turnout based on the various levels of spending in battleground states, mean expenditures (23,345 GRPs), expenditures one standard deviation unit above the mean (38,278 GRPs), and the maximum level of expenditures (45,763 GRPs) in these states were substituted in the model above for each state's actual level of spending. The turnout figures are the mean of the predicted state turnout weighted by the voting eligible population.

21. The data for this section are taken from Thomas Patterson, *The Vanishing Voter* (2003).

6

Winner-Take-All Elections,
Part II

Competition, Spending,
and Turnout in U.S. House Elections

In Chapter 5, I demonstrated that varying degrees of competition across states in the Electoral College result in varying turnout levels. In their efforts to win presidential elections, candidates and parties allocate their resources to the most competitive states and ignore the uncompetitive states. Given the small number of battleground states in any election, turnout is lower than it could be if all states were treated equally. This pattern should also be found in congressional elections. Representation in the U.S. House of Representatives is based on a system of 435 single-member districts elected through winner-take-all procedures. Some of these districts are competitive, while most are uncompetitive. In the competitive districts the outcome of an election is uncertain, and therefore the candidates, parties, and allied groups should expend whatever resources they have to win the election. As with the Electoral College, the increased campaign activity should translate into relatively high turnout. Conversely, in districts that are uncompetitive fewer resources should be distributed because the outcome of the election is certain, and as a result turnout should be lower than in the competitive districts. The remainder of this chapter will focus on the impact of district-level competitiveness on turnout in congressional elections.[1]

A Note on Turnout
in Midterm Elections

The starting point for any discussion of turnout in congressional elections is that turnout in midterm elections is substantially lower than turnout in presidential elections. Since 1960 the mean turnout in presidential elections is approximately 55 percent, while over the same period turnout in midterm elections is approximately 41 percent. One of the earliest and most insightful explanations for the low turnout in midterm elections is Campbell's (1960) "surge and decline" theory, which suggests that turnout in presidential elections is higher because in addition to core voters (regular voters), peripheral or marginal voters are brought to the polling place in response to the heightened visibility of the campaign. Midterm elections are relatively low visibility affairs and thus the less engaged marginal voters (occasional voters) refrain from voting and turnout is lower.

Franklin and Evans (2000) argue that turnout in congressional midterm elections is lower because they are "second order" elections that choose officials to a level of government that is not directly responsible for governing the nation, "but whose outcomes are structured entirely by considerations relevant to the outcomes of first order elections, which are directly responsible for the governance of the nation" (Franklin and Evans 2000, 97). Given that these elections are considered less important, fewer voters tend to show up. According to these authors the first order election in the United States is the presidential election and all lower elections, including midterm congressional elections, are second order elections. Given that Congress is the central lawmaking body in the U.S. system and an equal partner in the process with the president, congressional elections are not second order elections. Additionally, midterm elections have a substantial impact on the direction of policymaking in the United States because they determine who will control the Congress, the president's party or the opposition. However, the perception among most citizens is that the presidential election is the one that determines the policymaking direction of the country. Thus the media cover the presidential campaign more thoroughly and a greater percentage of citizens are brought into the electoral process, while midterms are treated as second order elections and turnout is therefore much lower.

Jackson (2000) found that the difference in visibility and campaign intensity between presidential and midterm elections has its greatest effect on the young and the mobile. In the low visibility midterm elections both groups find little reason to overcome the registration obstacles and thus do not turn out on Election Day. However, in the high visibility environment of presidential elections, both groups appear to be mobilized by the politicized environment of the national campaign and the campaign efforts of the two parties and their candidates. Within this context, these normally "nonvoting" groups find a reason to overcome the registration obstacles and show up to cast a ballot on Election Day (Jackson 2000).

It is unlikely that midterm elections will ever see the turnout level of presidential elections. However, variation in short-term campaign-specific forces such as the mobilization of the parties and candidates has a noticeable effect on turnout in congressional elections. The remainder of this chapter will focus on district-level turnout in the 2002 midterm U.S. House elections to explore the impact of district-level competitiveness on mobilization and turnout.

The Nature of Congressional Elections

The dominant characteristic of elections for the U.S. House of Representatives is the lack of competition. Since 1946 an average of 92 percent of House incumbents have won reelection (Jacobson 2004). This has led students of congressional elections to refer to the "incumbency advantage." The advantage House incumbents have in elections is a complex phenomenon comprising several components.

The first source of the incumbency advantage can be found in the institutional nature of the House of Representatives. For instance, the committee system allows members to specialize in policy areas beneficial to their local districts. While congressional members serving on committees to benefit their districts seems to fulfill their responsibilities as representatives, it also enables them to provide benefits to their districts, which proves useful when seeking reelection.[2] Additionally, party leadership has historically taken the position that reelection is the number one priority and thus members of Congress were encouraged to "vote their districts first" (Jacobson 2004; see also Mayhew 1974; Dodd and Sullivan 1981). Members are provided an array of benefits that they can use to get reelected. For example, each member is given a travel budget, personal staff, and free mail to constituents (the franking privilege). These benefits can be viewed as helping members stay in touch with their constituents; they also, however, aid in members' reelection efforts. The ability to connect with constituents allows members to "advertise" themselves to the district (Mayhew 1974). Each time a member returns home, sends a mass mailing to the district, or communicates in some way with a constituent, she is increasing her name recognition inside the district.

In addition to efforts to advertise themselves through personal contact and correspondence, congressional members also seek to claim credit for fulfilling the responsibilities of their jobs (Mayhew 1974). They can do this in two ways. First, congressional members engage in casework, or constituency service. Casework entails the member (actually the member's office) helping a constituent solve a problem with the federal bureaucracy. By doing this the member is able to take credit for helping constituents with the "overwhelming and inaccessible" federal bureaucracy. In his classic work *Congress: Keystone of the Washington Establishment*, Morris Fiorina argues that the growth in the federal government following World War II resulted in greater demands from citizens for help in dealing with problems with the federal government. Given that the congressional members could claim credit for helping constituents, Congress responded by adding to each member's personal staff, most of whom were assigned to dealing with constituent demands (Jacobson 2004).

Congressional incumbents can also claim credit for themselves by delivering federally funded projects to the district—pork barrel politics. In this way they demonstrate their effectiveness as congressional members to constituents. As Fiorina notes, large projects are highly visible and the economic impact on the district is obvious to most residents (Fiorina 1989). Because casework and pork projects are non-partisan, citizens come to view the member in personal terms as an incumbent who can deliver services to constituents and the district. Fiorina argues that as a result congressional members turn to casework and the pork barrel as a strategy for reelection, and thus incumbents overwhelmingly win reelection. While the empirical evidence for Fiorina's argument is mixed, the fact is that the ability to help constituents resolve problems with the bureaucracy and bring federally funded projects to the district are advantages that incumbents possess but challengers do not.[3]

The strongest reason for incumbents' overwhelming success in winning reelection is that the combination of resources available to incumbents discourages serious challengers, and thus most congressional incumbents face inexperienced, underfunded challengers in their reelection bids, and many face no opposition at all. Politicians, like people in other professions, seek to advance their careers. In American politics there is an unwritten but real hierarchy of offices starting at the local level and ending with the presidency. Individuals who seek a career in politics develop strategies to achieve their goals (Dodd 1985).[4] A lopsided loss to an incumbent can derail such plans, and consequently most quality challengers (those who have held elective office prior to the congressional race) refrain from challenging incumbents and instead make their bid for Congress in open seat races, or elections in which there is no incumbent (Jacobson 2004). For example, in 2002, 85 percent of the forty-six open seats had at least one challenger who had held prior elective office. Conversely, only 12 percent of 299 seats with an incumbent had a quality challenger.[5] Clearly, quality candidates chose open seats because of the substantially higher probability of winning.[6]

Finally, the other resource that can be brought to bear in an election is money. Incumbents can raise as much money as they need to wage a campaign. Generally, contributors (individuals and groups) will give money to the candidate who is perceived to have the greatest chance of winning, which in most cases is the incumbent. As Jacobson notes, contributors will "waste no money on sure losers but have no qualms about giving money to sure winners" (Jacobson 2004, 42). Additionally, the incumbent can count on the party organization to provide funds in a tight race. The controversy is whether or not spending in a campaign context actually helps the incumbent as much as the challenger.

Jacobson (1978, 1980, 1985, 1990) has demonstrated that the more money a challenger spends in an election campaign, the higher the percentage of the vote he or she receives. As noted above, however, contributors give money to those who have a good chance of winning, and thus the more competitive a challenger seems prior to the election, the more money he or she will receive from contributors. There is a circular relationship here that is difficult to disentangle. To have a chance of winning a congressional election, challengers need to spend a great deal of money. Jacobson (2004) found, for instance, that under average national conditions the minimum cost of a House campaign is $700,000; all of the thirty-seven challengers who defeated incumbents between 1996 and 2002 spent more than this.

Why is money so important to challengers? The answer to this question lies in the incumbency advantage explained above. Incumbents have a broad array of institutional resources that benefit their re-election bids. Most challengers for House elections do not have travel budgets, free mail, or a personal staff that has communicated with the district electorate for two years. The only way for a challenger to effectively compete with an incumbent is to overcome the disadvantage by spending large sums of money to get his or her name and message in front of the public.

Incumbents, on the other hand, appear to receive diminishing returns from their campaign spending. Jacobson has argued that the more money an incumbent spends the lower the percentage of the vote he or she receives. The reason for this is that the incumbent's level of spending is, in large part, a function of the challenger's. The more money a challenger spends, the more money an incumbent spends.

Therefore, higher levels of spending by an incumbent indicate a strong challenger and therefore a lower percentage of the vote to the incumbent. Green and Krasno (1988, 1990) and Erikson and Palfrey (1998) argue that when models for spending in House elections are properly estimated, spending by the incumbent has a significant and positive effect on the vote total. Although the impact of spending on the incumbent's electoral fortunes is controversial, clearly the stronger the challenge to the incumbent the greater the level of spending in a House race.

Quality Candidates, Open Seats, and Campaign Spending

As noted earlier, quality candidates are those who have previously held elective office.[7] They are generally stronger than nonquality candidates because their experience holding elective office and running in election campaigns gives them name recognition, an understanding of campaigns and electoral politics, and connections with influential people. Because quality candidates tend to be professional politicians who seek to climb up the political ladder, they tend to avoid challenging incumbents, or at least those perceived to reside in a safe district. Therefore, quality candidates tend to bide their time until they can run in a race with no incumbent, otherwise known as an open seat (Gaddie and Bullock 2000; Jacobson 2004), where their chances of winning are far greater (Jacobson 2004). Most open seats attract multiple quality candidates who compete for their party's nomination (Gaddie and Bullock 2000), and in many cases open seat elections include more than one quality candidate. For example, in the 2002 midterm elections 34 percent of open seat races involved two candidates who had held previous elective office.

Open seat races tend to be more competitive than races with an incumbent, although not all open races are competitive. Gaddie and Bullock (2000) found that between 1982 and 1988 roughly 37 percent of open seat races were won with less than 55 percent of the vote, while another 26 percent were won with between 55 and 60 percent of the total vote. The remaining 37 percent of races in this period were won with over 60 percent of the vote and thus were not competitive. The numbers were similar in the 2002 elections, with 30 percent of open seat races won with less than 55 percent of the vote and 22 percent of open seat races won with between 56 percent and 60 percent of the vote. While not universally competitive, open seat contests are nonetheless more competitive, as one would expect, than races with a sitting incumbent.

Open seat races tend to have higher levels of spending than races with an incumbent, due to their competitive nature. As noted above, contributors generally give money to candidates who have a good chance of winning, and thus candidates in open seat races tend to attract and spend larger amounts of money than nonincumbent candidates in races with a sitting incumbent. From 1972 to 2002 spending by nonincumbent candidates in open seats averaged over $500,000 per race (in 2000 dollars). Conversely, in districts in which the challenger's party received less than 45 percent in the previous election, nonincumbent candidates facing incumbents spent on average less than $200,000 per race (Jacobson 2004). Given the higher level of spending by candidates in open seat races, we would expect total spending in these races to be, on average, greater than in races with a sitting incumbent. For example, in 2002 the mean level of spending in the forty-six open seat races was $2,205,898, while races with an incumbent averaged $1,170,780.[8] Clearly the uncertainty and the relatively equal footing of the candidates in open seat races spur donors to contribute to these campaigns and the candidates to expend these resources in an effort to win the seat.

Gaddie and Bullock (2000) note that while open seat races are more competitive than incumbent races and more money is spent as a result, in most open seat races one candidate raises and spends more money than the other. This spending differential is related to whether or not there are one or two quality candidates in an open seat race. The mean spending difference between candidates in an open seat race with one quality candidate in 2002 was $935,755, while in open seat races with two candidates the mean spending difference was $673,644. The spending difference that Gaddie and Bullock note is still present; however, the difference is reduced by roughly 30 percent when there are two quality candidates in an open seat race rather than one. Therefore, mean total spending in races with two quality candidates should be higher than in races with one. In 2002 mean spending in open seat races was indeed greater in races with two quality candidates ($2,406,898 vs. $2,220,329), but the difference is a modest 8 percent.

The research on open seat races suggests three important patterns: (1) open seat races attract quality candidates, (2) those candidates raise and spend more money that nonincumbent candidates who challenge incumbents, and (3) open seat races are more competitive than races with an incumbent running for reelection. The literature on congressional elections illustrates the importance of competition in elections. Given that the more competitive a House election is the more money will be spent, turnout is also likely to be higher. In the next section we will explore the relationship between the nature of congressional elections and turnout.

Competition, Money, and Turnout

The relatively sparse research on turnout in House elections suggests that competition and spending in House races are positively related to district-level turnout (Caldeira, Patterson, and Markko 1985; Conway 1981; Cox and Munger 1989; Gilliam 1985; Jackson 1996). Cox and Munger (1989) examined those races in the 1982 midterm elections in which an incumbent faced opposition and found that close elections and high spending were associated with higher turnout in House elections. Their findings are important because when spending and other factors are held constant, the closeness of the election was significantly related to turnout, suggesting that some citizens appeared to be motivated to show up on Election Day because they believed their vote would be important to determining the outcome of the election. As discussed in Chapter 2, this is the central and most controversial premise of the calculus of voting. Thus Cox and Munger's study appears to support the notion that citizens are induced into voting in close elections because they think their vote matters. The authors conclude, however, that the observed relationship between the closeness of the election and turnout is more than likely a result of increased mobilization efforts on the part of the candidates and parties. In other words, close elections stimulate the candidates and parties to spend heavily and consequently turnout is high.

Cox and Munger, however, provide no empirical link for the hypothesized relationship between closeness, spending, and turnout. Jackson (1996) argues that Cox and Munger are "implicitly" making a path analytic argument when they state that rather than directly stimulating turnout, as the instrumental voting argument suggests, close elections indirectly lead to higher levels of turnout because they stimulate the campaigns to spend whatever resources are necessary (or that they have) to win an election, which then leads to higher turnout. Jackson argues that in order to appropriately model turnout in House elections we need to link the empirical literature on House elections with the turnout literature. He proposes a path model that incorporates the quality of the candidates involved in the race, the level of campaign spending, the closeness of the race, and turnout.

Figure 6.1 below presents a modification of the model presented by Jackson. Given the higher levels of competition in open seat races and the subsequently higher level of spending in these races, it is reasonable to assume that turnout in these races should be higher as a result of the increased spending. Because of this possibility, the model below is modified to incorporate the impact of open seats on district-level turnout. Jackson's model, based heavily in congressional literature on the impact of challengers in House elections, emphasizes challenger quality and spending. His framework begins by explaining the source of challenger quality. He argues that the greater the proportion of the vote that the challenger's party received in the previous election, the greater the likelihood that a quality candidate would challenge an incumbent in the current election. This is because qual-

FIG 6.1   Path Model of Congressional Turnout

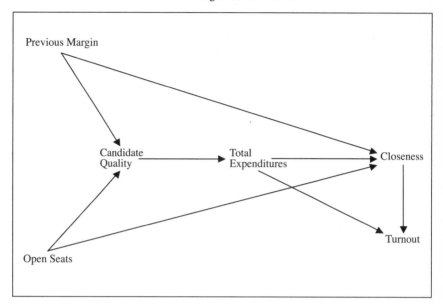

ity candidates are more likely to challenge an incumbent when the district is competitive.

Additionally, Jackson considers the party of the challenger based on the notion that if short-term national political tides favor the challenger's party, there is a greater chance of a quality challenger facing an incumbent. Given that we are incorporating open seats into the model, adjustments need to be made to these two variables. Rather than using the percentage of the vote received by the challenger's party in the previous election (there is no challenger in open seats), the model in Figure 6.1 uses the closeness of the outcome in the previous election. The logic here is that the more competitive the previous election the greater the chances of a challenger (or a candidate in an open seat) winning the current election. Because open seats don't have challengers, the modified model also omits the variable for the challenger's party. In its place the model includes a variable for whether or not there is an open seat. Given the discussion in the previous section, open seats are more likely to include at least one quality candidate.

The model in the first column of Table 6.1 presents the OLS (ordinary least squares) estimates for candidate quality in the 2002 midterm elections.[9] The coefficient for the margin in the previous election is significant and negative, suggesting that the greater the margin of victory in the previous election the less likely the current election involved a quality candidate, or, conversely, the closer the previous election, the greater the likelihood that the current election included a quality candidate. The coefficient for the open seat dummy variable is significant and positive, indicating that open seat races were significantly more likely to involve a quality candidate than races with an incumbent. Clearly the competitive districts, either those that were marginal in the last election and thus gave the challenger a better chance of winning or open seats that have no incumbent are inducements for quality candidates to run for a House seat.

Jackson's model posits that the level of incumbent and challenger expenditures in a House race is positively related to the proportion of the vote that the challenger's party received in the previous party and the quality of the challenger. The modified model in Table 6.1 uses total House expenditures as a surrogate for incumbent and challenger expenditures in order to accommodate open seat races, which do not have incumbents and challengers. The logic of the argument remains the same as Jackson's, however. The more competitive the race in the previous election, the greater the level of total expenditures we should expect in the 2002 election.[10] Open seats should receive higher levels of spending than races with incumbents, and races with quality candidates should also experience higher levels of spending. The second column in Table 6.1 presents the OLS estimates for total spending in House races in 2002. The findings are also consistent with Jackson's model in that races with quality candidates have significantly higher spending than races without quality candidates. Open seat races also have significantly higher spending than races with an incumbent, and the closer the race in the 2000 election, the higher the spending in 2002.

Jackson argues that the literature on congressional elections indicates that greater spending by a challenger leads to a closer election. Additionally, higher levels of spending by the challenger lead to

TABLE 6.1   OLS Estimates of Candidate Quality, Total Expenditures, and Closeness of Outcome in the 2002 Midterm Elections

	Candidate Quality	Total Expenditures	Closeness of Outcome
Previous margin	−.004*	−.01*	463.94*
	(.001)	(.002)	(77.71)
Open seats	.734*	.469*	−14497.22*
	(.001)	(.134)	(5232.78)
Quality		.371*	19.51
		(.097)	(3818.96)
Total expenditures			−13738.92*
			(2210.06)
Constant	.290*	1.095*	53365.08*
Adjusted R^2	.305	.315	.360

*$p<.01$
standard errors are in parentheses

higher levels by the incumbent, which also leads to a closer outcome. The quality of the challenger and the strength of the challenger's party in the last election can be expected to affect the closeness of the election. Jackson's OLS model found that in 1990 (a midterm election) the only variables to have a significant impact on the closeness of the outcome were the strength of the challenger's party and the level of challenger spending.[11] In Figure 6.1 the closeness of the challenger in the 2002 election is replaced by the closeness of the outcome of the election, but the logic is the same as Jackson's.[12] The closeness of the election should be in large part influenced by the level of expenditures, the closeness of the previous election, and whether or not the election was for an open seat.

The final column in Table 6.1 presents the OLS estimates for the closeness of election outcomes in 2002. Open seat races were significantly related to the closeness of the election, with the raw vote difference in open seats being on average 14,497 votes smaller than in races with an incumbent. The margin of victory in the previous election is also significantly related to the closeness of the election. A one standard deviation unit (19 points) increase in the margin of victory in the 2000 election resulted in an increase of 8,797 votes. As expected, the greater the total expenditures in 2002 House elections, the closer the outcome of the election. A one standard deviation unit increase (.71) in the log of total expenditures resulted in a 13,738 vote decrease in the raw vote difference in the closeness of the election in 2002. As with Jackson's models, the quality of the challenger is not directly related to the closeness of the election.

The models in Table 6.1 illustrate nicely how the competition level of House districts works through candidate quality and expenditures to influence the closeness of an election. As with Jackson, the results verify the literature on congressional elections. The final step in this analysis is to estimate turnout in 2002. Table 6.2 presents the OLS estimates for district-level turnout in 2002. The model includes a variety of contextual and campaign-specific variables known to be related to turnout. The variables of interest for this analysis are the closeness of the election outcome and total House expenditures. Consistent with Jackson (1996) and Cox and Munger (1989), the closeness of the election is significantly related to district-level turnout. A one standard deviation unit decrease in the closeness of the election (29,369 votes) increased turnout levels on average eight percentage points. Total House expenditures are also significantly related to turnout, with a one unit increase in the log of total expenditures increasing turnout by approximately one percentage point.

The results in Table 6.2 indicate that both closeness and expenditures are significantly related to turnout. Based on the discussion above, we know that closeness is, in large part, a function of expenditures, quality, margin of victory in the previous election, and whether or not the election is for an open seat. Because of this, we need to examine the indirect effects of all of these variables on turnout. Indirect effects are calculated by multiplying the coefficients from Table 6.1 with the coefficients for closeness and expenditures in Table 6.2. For example, by influencing the closeness of the outcome of the election, total expenditures in a House race increased turnout by about one percentage point ($-13738.92 * -.0000008 = .01$). In other words, cam-

TABLE 6.2   OLS Estimates of District-Level Turnout in 2002 Midterm Elections

	Unstandardized Coefficients	*Standard Errors*
Education	.311**	.072
Income	−.000003**	.000
Residential mobility	.04	.035
Urbanization	−.04	.028
Population density	−.000002**	.000
Percentage sixty-five	.172*	.074
Percentage black	−.133**	.024
Percentage Latino	−.228**	.025
Northeast	−.0008	.009
Midwest	.02**	.007
West	.002	.009
Closing date	−.002**	.000
Governor's race	.09**	.013
Senate race	.006	.014
Governor's race* margin	.03	.036
Senate race* margin	−.03	.021
Governor's race* spending	−.05**	.009
Senate race* spending	.03**	.009
Closeness	−.0000008*	.000
Closeness squared	.0000000001**	.000
Total expenditures	.01**	.004
Constant	.394**	
Adjusted R^2	.76	

*p<.05; **p<.01

paigns with high levels of spending tend to be close, and as a result of the closeness and intensity of the elections, turnout is high. As the co-efficient for expenditures in Table 6.2 suggests, campaign expenditures not only lead to higher turnout by leading to a close race but also lead directly to higher turnout by reducing the costs of participation for potential voters. Given this direct effect, we need to calculate the total effect of spending on turnout by adding the direct effect in Table 6.2

(.01) with the indirect effect noted above (.01). Therefore the total effect of campaign expenditures on district level turnout is approximately two percentage points (.01 + .01 = .02).

As Jackson and others have noted, and the estimates in Table 6.1 indicate, House races with at least one quality candidate experience higher levels of spending than races without a quality candidate, and therefore the presence of at least one quality candidate has an indirect effect on turnout working through expenditures and closeness. We can calculate the indirect effect of quality on turnout by multiplying the coefficient for quality in the expenditures model in Table 6.1 (.371) with expenditures coefficient in the closeness model in Table 6.1 (−13738.92) and the coefficient for closeness in the turnout model in Table 6.2 (−.0000008). Based on this calculation, the indirect effect of quality on turnout is roughly one-half of one percentage point. As already noted, quality candidates are more likely to enter an open seat race than challenge an incumbent; therefore, we would expect open seat races to work through candidate quality to indirectly affect turnout. The indirect effect of open seats on turnout due to the presence of quality candidates is about one-third of a percentage point (.734 * .371 * −13738 * −.0000008). The indirect effect of the margin of victory in the previous election had a very minimal effect on turnout.

Open seats also have an impact on turnout that works independent of quality. For instance, due to increases in the level of spending, open seat races have turnout levels one-half of one percentage higher than non-open seat races (.469 * −13738.92 * −.0000008). The estimates presented in Table 6.1 also indicate that the outcome of open seat races tends to be closer than races with an incumbent, and thus these races have turnout levels one percentage point higher than races with an incumbent due to the closeness of the election, even when controlling for expenditures (−14497.22 * −.0000008).

The literature on congressional elections and the data presented in this chapter suggest a strong relationship between an open seat, campaign expenditures, closeness of the outcome, and turnout, and thus examining the relationship between these variables simultaneously is

FIG 6.2 Predicted National Turnout Across Levels of Competition and Spending

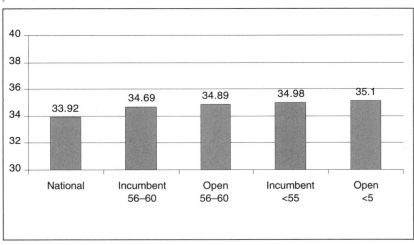

informative. Figure 6.2 presents the predicted turnout by levels of competitiveness and whether or not the race was for an open seat. The national turnout predicted by the model is 33.92.[13] In races with an incumbent in which the winner received between 56 and 60 percent of the vote, predicted turnout was approximately 34.69 percent, and in open seat races with this level of competitiveness turnout was 34.89 percent. In both cases turnout increased by just shy of one percentage point. The other two categories are for incumbent and open seat races in which the winner won with less than 56 percent of the vote. In both of these types of races turnout increased by just over one percentage point. The data presented in Figure 6.2 suggest few differences between incumbent and open seat races independent of competition and spending. Clearly the effect of spending and competition on turnout is modest, but the results presented here do suggest that in competitive elections in which the campaigns spend relatively large amounts of resources, the open seat turnout is increased.

A key point of the analysis in this chapter is that competitive House elections, particularly open seat races, tend to attract quality candidates who spend large amounts of money. Following the decennial reapportionment of the House, it is not unusual for redistricting to produce a handful of races in which two incumbents are forced to face off in a race for one new House seat. These races should be competitive. They include two candidates who are sitting members of the House of Representatives. Each candidate can bring the incumbency advantage to bear, and both candidates should be well funded. The competitiveness of these races should induce the candidates to spend whatever resources are necessary to win. Because of this, we would expect turnout to exceeed that in races with an incumbent or even an open seat race.

In 2002 there were four House races in which two incumbents faced each other. The patterns discussed above were evident in these four races. Figure 6.3 presents the mean level of spending and closeness across three categories of races in 2002: (1) one incumbent, (2) open seat, (3) two incumbents. As expected, the four races with two incumbents experienced substantially higher levels of spending that the other two types of races. For example, the mean level of spending in the four two-incumbent races was $4,225,965. The race with lowest spending of the four ($3,142,378) had a spending level substantially higher than the mean level of spending for open seat and one-incumbent races. As the discussion in this chapter demonstrated, higher levels of spending in House races lead to closer outcomes. The data presented in Figure 6.4 indicate that races with two incumbents are also much closer than the open seat races and races with one incumbent. The mean closeness of the outcome of two-incumbent races is 28,818 votes, while in open seat races the mean is 32,569 votes, and in races with one incumbent the mean outcome is 60,781 votes. Clearly races with two incumbents experience substantially higher levels of spending and are much closer than other races. Because of this we can reasonably expect turnout to be higher in these races. This appears to be the case. The mean level of turnout in the four two-incumbent races in 2002 was 43 percent, substantially higher than the mean of 37 percent for both one-incumbent and open seat races. Clearly the intensity of the campaign and the high visibility of a House election with two incumbents facing off for one seat leads to higher turnout.

FIG 6.3   Total Expenditures in One-Incumbent, Open Seat, and Two-Incumbent Races

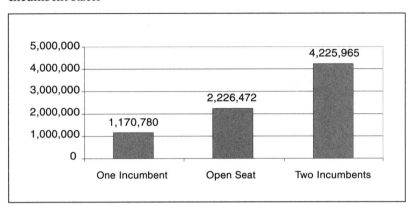

FIG 6.4   Closeness in One-Incumbent, Open Seat, and Two-Incumbent Races

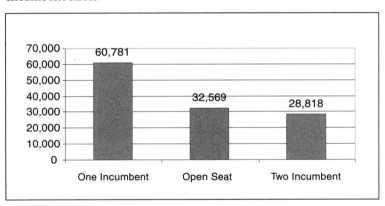

The discussion and analysis presented in this chapter illustrate the impact of competition on turnout in congressional races.[14] As noted earlier, congressional elections are characterized by a low level of competitiveness. In 2002 eighty-two incumbents ran unopposed. In races where the incumbent faces a challenger, it is usually someone who is inexperienced and underfunded, which leaves a relatively small subset of competitive races. In 2002 fifty-three races with an incumbent were decided by less than ten percentage points; there were forty-nine open seat races and four races with two incumbents. Given this relatively small subset of races in which the competition and spending levels are sufficient to attract voters to the polls, it is not surprising that turnout historically is low in congressional elections. Franklin and Evans (2000) argue that turnout would be higher in midterm elections if the number of competitive congressional districts were higher. The analysis presented in this chapter suggests that greater competitiveness in congressional races would lead to modestly higher turnout levels. However, given the inherent advantages that incumbents possess in the electoral process, it is unlikely that competition levels in House elections will improve in the foreseeable future.

Notes

1. Gary Jacobson supplied most of the data used in this chapter to the author, who is responsible for all opinions, findings, and conclusions or recommendations. The data concerning district-level demographics were taken from the U.S. Census Bureau's 108th Congressional District Summary Files.

2. The committee system allows members of Congress to obtain benefits for their districts, which aids reelection efforts. However, members of Congress are concerned with more than reelection. They seek to acquire power and influence within the institution. Committees (or at least certain committees) enable members to earn the respect of their peers and gain and exercise power. Because of this, committees are especially attractive for members in the "quest for power" (Dodd 1977).

3. See Serra (1994, 1995) and Serra and Cover (1995) for empirical examinations of the effects of casework on incumbent evaluations of congressional electoral outcomes.

4. Dodd argues that while reelection is an important aspect of each House member's career strategy, it is not the sole variable in his or her calculus. Instead, as members seek to gain influence within the institution and build a career, they need to master four types of resources: (1) reelection, (2) policy development, (3) institutional influence, and (4) organizational control. Reelection is the first stage in a career path within the institution of Congress.

5. Incumbents who were not opposed in 2002 are excluded from this analysis.

6. Jacobson (2004) found that between 1946 and 2002 roughly 50 percent of the candidates for open seats had held prior elective office while only 25 percent of candidates challenging incumbents had held elective office prior to running for Congress.

7. Other researchers have opted for a more complex definition of quality. Krasno and Green (1988), for instance, argue that quality comprises two components: (1) attractiveness (How appealing is the candidate to voters?) and (2) political skill (Does the candidate have the skills necessary to run an effective campaign?). Based on these components, the authors built a scale that included a series of items used to measure attractiveness and skill. The analysis in this chapter will follow the lead of Jacobson and others and measure quality as a simple dichotomous variable for whether or not the candidate had held political office.

8. This figure is based on incumbents facing a challenger. The mean for all races with incumbents, including those in which the incumbent faced no challenger, is $1,048,783.

9. Given that the variable for the presence of an open seat is dichotomous, the appropriate estimation technique is either logit or probit analysis. However, as Jackson notes, the calculation and comparison of path coefficients necessitates the use of OLS in all models in this analysis. The results of the logistic regression are essentially the same as those for the OLS analysis: both the coefficients for open seats and closeness in the previous election are significant and the signs are the same.

10. The competitiveness of the previous election is measured as the vote margin in the 1998 midterm House elections.

11. In 1988 the challenger's party (coded 1 as Democrat) was significant and negatively related to closeness of the outcome in House races. The negative sign indicates that Democrat House challengers did not fare well in 1988 due to short-term trends, including a presidential race in which the Democrat nominee, Michael Dukakis, was soundly defeated by Republican George H.W. Bush.

12. Closeness of the challenger is measured as the raw vote difference between the challenger and the incumbent. Closeness of the outcome is measured as the raw vote difference between the winner and loser of the election.

13. This estimate is calculated as expected turnout $_{2002}$ = .394 + (college percentage * .311) + (per capita income * −.000003) + (residential mobility * .04) + (urbanization * −.04) + (population density * −.000002) + (percentage

sixty-five * .172) + (Black * --.133) + (Latino * -.228) + (North * -.0008) + (Midwest * .02) + (West * .002) + (closing date * -.002) + (gubernatorial race * .09) + (Senate race * .006) + (gubernatorial race X margin * .03) + (Senate race X margin * -.03) + (gubernatorial race X log of gubernatorial expenditures * -.05) + (Senate race X log of senatorial expenditures * .03) + (closeness * -.0000008) + (closeness squared * .0000000001) + (total expenditures * .01). In order to calculate the base national turnout, the above model multiplied each state's actual media spending and candidate visits by the respective coefficients for media spending and candidate visits. To calculate turnout based on the various levels of competition and spending, levels of expenditures for two different levels of competition (races won with 55 percent or less of the vote and races won with between 56 and 60 percent of the vote) were substituted for all races. The turnout figures are the mean of the predicted state turnout weighted by the voting eligible population.

14. Jackson (1996) notes that during presidential elections the stimulating effects of congressional elections are overridden by the intensity and visibility of presidential campaigns. Also see Jackson 1997.

7

The Separation of Powers

Divided Government, Responsiveness, Accountability, and Turnout

In Chapters 5–6 we examined how winner-take-all elections constrain turnout by shaping the campaign strategies of parties and candidates and thereby affect citizens' behavior. In this chapter we will examine the impact of the central institution of the American system—the separation of powers—on turnout. Rather than affecting turnout by shaping the behavior of political elites, the separation of powers works to convince citizens that government does not respond to citizen demands. Consequently many believe that voting in elections makes no difference in the policy outputs of government and choose to stay home on Election Day (Franklin 2004; Franklin and Hirczy de Mino 1998). The core concept behind this argument is "executive responsiveness," or the ability of the executive to respond to the demands of the voting electorate (Banks 1997; Franklin 2004; Powell 2000). A nation with a high level of executive responsiveness is able to translate the preferences of the voting population into policy outcomes. In a nation with a low level of responsiveness the executive has difficulty doing so. Turnout tends to be higher in systems with high levels of executive responsiveness because citizens believe that their preferences will be translated into policy if their party wins control of the government. When the executive has difficulty translating electoral demands into policy outputs, citizens come to believe that elections are not linked to policy. As a result, elections are less salient to many citizens and turnout is lower (Franklin 1996, 2004).

The United States is considered to have a low level of executive responsiveness (Banks 1997; Franklin 2004) stemming from the system of separation of powers. Because the lawmaking power in the United States resides with Congress, a victory in the presidential election, while giving the president the ability to shape the executive branch, gives the president no power to implement his policy agenda. Therefore the president must have the consent of Congress to carry out the policy proposals on which he campaigned. But even when one party controls both houses of Congress, its ability to enact its agenda depends largely on the president because all bills must be signed into law by the president. In either case, an electoral victory does not necessarily translate into policy outputs. Because of this, elections are less salient to citizens because they come to believe elections do not result in policy outputs (Franklin 1996, 2004). In addition, the separation of powers reduces citizens' ability to assess governmental performance and thus reduces their ability to assess credit or blame for past performance or lack of performance. Given the reduced responsiveness, blurred accountability, and lowered electoral saliency due to the separation of powers, we would expect the United States to have lower levels of turnout than nations without separation of powers systems (Franklin 2004).

In stark contrast to the U.S. system of strict separation of powers is the typical parliamentary system, such as Great Britain. The winning party is given not only the right to control the parliament and thus pass laws but also the right to form a government and shape the executive with its members. Once in control of the parliament, the government (the majority party) can pass and implement its policy agenda with relative ease.[1] The responsiveness of this system is easy to identify. The party that wins the most votes takes control of both the lawmaking and implementation arms of the governmental apparatus (they are essentially one in the same) and thus is able to translate the preferences of its supporters into policies. In these systems, then, citizens come to believe that elections produce substantive policy outputs and therefore believe that voting in elections is worthwhile.[2]

Since the late 1940s many American political scientists have argued that the United States would benefit from the responsible party model (RPM), similar to that of the British parliamentary system.[3] Proponents of RPM argue that governance in the United States would be more effective with two strong parties that present the electorate with clear party choices, and a party that carries out its agenda once it wins control of government. If this were the case, turnout would likely be higher since citizens would see voters' preferences translated into policy, as in most parliamentary systems. However, the presence of the separation of powers increases the difficulty of implementing an agenda and thus the RPM is difficult to achieve in the United States.

Divided Government and Policymaking in the United States

As Franklin (2004) notes, the United States is the only nation with a true separation of powers system and one of two nations with voluntary voter registration.[4] Because of these unique institutional arrangements, comparative analysis is difficult. However, we can examine the impact of the separation of powers on turnout by examining divided government across time. When one party controls the presidency and both Houses of Congress, policymaking should be facilitated because all three institutions are controlled by people who "are on the same team" and thus agree generally as to what direction policy should take. Additionally, accountability is heightened because members of the party in control should find it difficult to blame the other party for failures, scandals, and so on (Franklin 1998, 2004). This is as close as the United States can come to responsible party government. In contrast, when control of the legislative and executive branches is divided between the two parties, the direction that policy will take is blurred and accountability is greatly weakened, since each branch can blame the other for the perceived failures (Franklin 1998, 2004; see also Fiorina 1996; Mayhew 1991). If divided government does interfere with policymaking and accountability, many citizens will come to believe that little is at stake in elections because the winner has limited ability to shape the policy direction of the government. When each branch is controlled by a different party, the information costs associated with assessing governmental performance are dramatically increased for citizens, thus increasing the costs associated with voting. The belief that not much is at stake in elections and the increased information costs together should lead to lower levels of turnout (Franklin 2004). Examining the impact of divided government on turnout from 1840 to 1992, Franklin and Hirzcy de Mino (1998) found that turnout was lower during periods of divided government than during periods of unified government. For every four years of divided government turnout decreased 1.96 percentage points. The impact is cumulative, and therefore after eight years of divided government we can expect a decline in turnout of 3.92 points and after twelve years (there was no period of divided government longer than 12 years) turnout should decline by 5.88 points (Franklin 2004; Franklin and Hirzcy de Mino 1998). Divided government clearly has an impact on turnout in American elections. The task we face is to provide empirical evidence linking the presence of divided government with citizen attitudes toward government responsiveness and turnout.

The Impact of Divided Government on Governmental Policymaking

Does divided government actually affect the ability of the government to respond to citizen demands? Central to Franklin's argument is the notion that the separation of powers is less responsive to policy demands of electorates than parliamentary systems, and that divided government exacerbates this lack of responsiveness. Because of this, citizens tend to view the government as nonresponsive to citizen demands and don't expect elections to have an impact on policy outputs and consequently abstain from voting. Another key point in Franklin's argument is that during periods of divided control citizens' ability to accurately assess governmental performance is reduced and therefore the costs of information acquisition are increased. Thus it is hardly surprising that turnout is lower during periods of divided government.

There is little question about reduced accountability during periods of divided government. There is considerable controversy, however, as to whether or not divided government hinders the ability of the national government to produce substantive policy. Examining policy outputs from 1947 through 1990, Mayhew (1991) found that the number of significant pieces of legislation enacted did not substantively differ between periods of divided government and periods of unified government. This seminal work challenged the commonly held belief that divided government hinders policy production. Mayhew suggests that partisan control of the legislative and executive branches has little impact on the amount of important legislation enacted by the government. Instead, as with most social and political phenomena, there are several factors that influence the degree of policy produced, such as the electoral incentive for congressional members to push legislation through Congress, the leadership abilities of the president, and the tendency of broad coalitions to form in order to solve problems. Forces outside of Washington can also affect policymaking. Unexpected events such as 9/11 can force action in a given policy area. Additionally, issues may arise that cut across the traditional party divide and thus transcend partisan cleavages in government. Finally, several scholars have noted that "moods" for policymaking develop in the American electorate, and policymaking increases in response to demands from the public (Mayhew 1991).[5] All in all, Mayhew presents a forceful argument that challenges the view that divided control of government should hinder the ability of government to produce substantive policy.[6]

The most direct counter to Mayhew's work came from Kelly (1993a,b), who argues that the pattern (or nonpattern) Mayhew found was in large part determined by his definition of "important" policies as those that (1) were deemed as important or innovative at the time of passage or (2) were deemed important or innovative retrospectively by historians or analysts. A policy did not have to meet both criteria to be included in the list. Kelly argues that a truly innovative policy would be one considered important at the time of passage and retrospectively. Using this standard, Kelly found that periods of unified government did indeed produce more innovative policies than periods of divided government.[7] In recent years several pieces of research have suggested that policymaking is negatively affected by divided government. For example, Edwards, Barrett, and Peake (1997) examined important pieces of legislation that were defeated, since the core argument is that divided government hinders the ability of the government to enact substantive policy. They found that during periods of divided government presidents were more likely to oppose legislation, and significant legislation fail to be enacted.

Coleman (1999) looks at the unified/divided government debate through the lens of responsiveness. He argues that the true question is not whether unified government produces more legislative enactments than divided government, but whether or not government is more responsive to majorities during periods of unified government. For example, if a majority of the electorate desires legislative activity, then a responsive government is one that is active. Conversely, if the mood of the electorate is subdued in terms of its desire to see policy enacted, a responsive government will produce less policy. Coleman argues that unified government is more likely to be responsive to the will of the majority than divided government, but not necessarily more productive. Using the Mayhew and Kelly's classifications of important legislation, as well as the Edwards, Barrett, and Peake's measures of policy failures, Coleman found that unified government produced more policy enactments, and policy failures were greater during periods of divided government. However, partisan control of government had an impact on policy outputs. For instance, unified governments controlled by Democrats increase the number of policy enactments, while unified governments controlled by Republicans decrease the number of policy enactments. In terms of responsiveness to the desires of the electorate, Coleman found that when the public mood is liberal and the majority of the electorate desires an active government, unified government increases the number of enactments and decreases the number of failures. The last finding suggests that unified government is more responsive to public desires than divided government, and it is consistent with Franklin's argument that divided government (and, more broadly, separation of powers systems) is less responsive to public demands than unified government. In the remainder of this chapter we will focus on citizen attitudes and divided government and how this relationship affects turnout.

Divided Government, Citizen Attitudes, and Turnout

As Franklin points out, because of the fragmentation of power and conflict between branches inherent to separation of powers, the U.S. system is less responsive to demands from the electorate than most parliamentary systems (Franklin 2004, Franklin and Hirczy de Mino 1998). Franklin asserts that because the separation of powers (and more specifically divided government) is less responsive, many citizens come to believe that elections have little to no impact on actual policy outcomes and thus refrain from voting. The key to Franklin's argument is citizen attitudes, and a full treatment of the relationship between divided government (and the separation of powers) and turnout needs to examine the impact of divided government on citizen attitudes. Franklin and Hirczy de Mino's (1998) work was limited in its ability to examine the relationship between divided government, citizen attitudes, and turnout because their time frame ranged from 1840 through 1992. Public opinion data from the nineteenth century are not available; high-quality, comparable data were not available until 1948 with the implementation of the first American National Election Study (NES) conducted by the Center for Political Research at the University of Michigan. Because of the prevalence of divided government in the postwar era and the implementation of the NES every two years since 1948, we can explore whether or not the presence of divided control of the federal government has an impact on citizen attitudes toward politics and government in general.

Using the 1948–2002 NES cumulative file, I will first identify measurable attitudes that should be affected by divided government and are related to the probability of voting.[8] As explained above, the key concept in Franklin's discussion of the separation of powers and divided government is responsiveness. If the government is indeed less responsive to the electorate's demands during periods of divided government, then many citizens will likely believe that it is unresponsive. *External efficacy* refers to the citizens' belief "about the responsiveness of governmental authorities and institutions to citizen demands" (Niemi, Craig, and Mattei 1991).[9] If divided government does affect the responsiveness of the government (or at least citizen perceptions of the responsiveness of the government), then a noticeable number of citizens during these periods should have lower levels of external efficacy than during periods of unified government. As noted, accountability is also a key to this argument. If citizens have problems assessing governmental performance, then it is likely that many will come to believe that the government is not responsive to citizen demands.

Citizens who believe that the government is not responsive to the demands of the electorate will likely turn away from politics. If a citizen believes that elections have little impact on politics, it would be rational for him or her to not pay attention to politics and government. Since 1960 the NES has asked two questions gauging citizens' attention to (1) the current campaign and (2) governmental affairs in general. Both questions can be classified under the phrase *interest in politics*. As with external efficacy, it is likely that citizens will have lower levels of interest in politics during periods of divided government than during periods of unified government. *Political knowledge* is related to interest in politics as well as the presence of divided government. Bennett and Bennett (1993) and Nicholson and Segura (1999) found that citizens participating in the NES during periods of divided government were less likely to correctly name the party that controlled the U.S. House of Representatives than respondents during periods of unified government. The fragmentation of power and the lowered ability of citizens to assess accountability inherent to divided government increases the information costs for most citizens (relative to periods of unified government), and therefore many citizens' knowledge of government decreases. Finally, an individual's *strength of partisanship*, or the degree to which a person identifies with one of the two major political parties, should also be related to partisan control of government. If the government is characterized by partisan conflict (as is likely during periods of divided government) and citizens also have difficulty assessing accountability along partisan lines, a noticeable number of citizens will likely view the parties in negative terms (Craig 1985, 1987) or from a position of neutrality (Wattenberg 1996). Because of this, we should see lower levels of partisan identification during periods of divided government.

All of the above concepts are related to Franklin's argument concerning government responsiveness during periods of divided government and how that affects turnout. If, as appears to be the case, the federal government is less responsive to the demands of the electorate and less accountable, then the variables described above should decline during periods of divided government. Given that all of these variables are associated with a higher probability of voting, lower levels of these attitudes should lead to a lower probability of voting. We now have a more complete model of Franklin's argument concerning divided government and turnout. During periods of divided government, the fragmentation of power and difficulty in assessing governmental performance are exacerbated by the partisan conflict that accompanies divided government. The government becomes less responsive to the mood of the public and accountability is blurred. Consequently citizens' external efficacy, interest in politics, political knowledge, and strength of partisanship decline, and there is a modest but noticeable decline in turnout.

Table 7.1 presents the difference between unified and divided government respondents in the probability of giving a particular response to the questions measuring external efficacy, interest in campaigns and public affairs, strength of partisan identification, and political knowledge.[10] All of these variables are significantly and negatively related to divided government, which means that during periods of divided government we see a significant decline in these important attitudes. The first section of the table presents the probability of a respondent scoring low, medium, or high on the external efficacy index.[11] Given that external efficacy index indicates the degree to which an individual believes that the government is responsive to the electorate, it is crucial to Franklin's argument that because separation of powers systems, and divided government in particular, are not as responsive as the typical parliamentary system, citizens should come to believe that government is not responsive to the desires of the electorate. The probabilities presented in Table 7.1 suggest that Franklin is correct. The difference between divided and unified government respondents in the probability of scoring low on the external efficacy index is three percentage points, indicating that respondents during periods of divided government are more likely to have low levels of external efficacy than respondents during periods of unified government. Conversely, the negative sign (–.06) in the cell for high external efficacy indicates that divided government respondents have a six percentage point lower probability of having a high level of external efficacy than unified government respondents. Based on these data, it appears that during periods of divided government citizens are less likely to believe that the government is responsive to citizen demands.

Both Bennett and Bennett (1993) and Nicholson and Segura (1999) found that during periods of divided government respondents were significantly less likely to correctly identify the party that held the majority of seats in the House of Representatives. The probabilities presented in the second row in Table 7.1 are similar to the findings of the authors noted above. The difference between divided government respondents and unified government respondents in incorrectly identifying the majority party in the House of Representatives is eight percentage points, which indicates that respondents during periods of unified government had an eight point greater likelihood of correctly identifying the majority party. Respondents during periods of divided government were eight points less likely than unified respondents to correctly identify the majority party. By weakening citizens' ability to assess governmental performance and thus blurring accountability, divided control of government creates an environment in which citizens

TABLE 7.1   Differential Probability of Voting Between Unified and Divided Government Respondents Based on Political Attitudes

	Low	Medium	High
External Efficacy	.03	.03	−.06

	Correct	Incorrect
Political Knowledge	.08	−.08

	Not Much Interested	Somewhat Interested	Very Interested
Interest in Campaign	.02	.02	−.04

	Hardly at All	Only Now and Then	Some of the Time	Most of the Time
Interest in Public Affairs	.005	.01	.004	−.02

	Independent	Leaner	Weak Partisan	Strong Partisan
Strength of Partisanship	.007	.01	.0009	−.02

Source: National Elections Study Cumulative File 1952–2002, Center for Political Studies, University of Michigan. The logistic coefficients from which these probabilities were calculated can be found in Appendix C.

have greater difficulty identifying even something as basic as which party controls the House of Representatives.

The next two entries in Table 7.1 are for the difference in the probabilities for *interest in the current campaign* and *interest in public affairs.* During periods of divided government respondents were slightly more likely to state that they were "not much interested" in the current campaign (.01) and less likely to state that they were "very much interested" (−.04). In terms of interest in general public affairs, there is little difference between divided government respondents and unified government respondents, although divided respondents are two points less likely to state that they follow governmental and public affairs "most of the time." Franklin and Hirzcy de Mino argue that during periods of divided government citizens come to believe that elections don't have a substantive impact on policy outcomes. The lowered interest in campaigns during these periods likely reflects this lowered sense that elections matter. Given the lack of responsiveness and the blurred lines of accountability during periods of divided government, citizens' interest in political affairs should decline as they come to see government and politics as distant.

Finally, partisan identification can also be directly affected by divided government. Given the blurred accountability and partisan conflict characteristic of divided government, some citizens are likely to (1) blame the political parties for the state of governmental affairs and thus turn away from the parties (Craig 1985a,b, 1987) or (2) view the two major parties in neutral terms (Wattenberg 1996). A good measure of this is whether or not citizens' partisan identification decreases during these periods. Based on the logic presented in this chapter, we would expect that during periods of divided government citizens would have weakened attachments to the two major political parties and even claim to be independents. Table 7.1 suggests that there is small impact of divided government on citizens' strength of party identification. There is no substantive difference between divided and unified respondents in the likelihood of claiming to be a "pure independent." However, there is a two point lower probability of claiming to be a "strong partisan" for respondents during periods of divided government. The results presented in Table 7.1 suggest that Franklin's argument is essentially correct: during periods of divided government citizens have lower levels of external efficacy and other important attitudes toward government and politics. The next step is to link these attitudes to the probability of voting.

Based on the discussion in Chapter 2 of the various models that seek to explain turnout, we can identify four groups of predictors to build a comprehensive model of the probability that an individual will cast a ballot in an election. The first, the legal environment, mainly registration laws (see Chapter 3), restricts access to the ballot and thus has a strong impact on the probability of voting. The second, demographic characteristics (education, income, race, age, gender, region), predicts the probability of voting due to differences in resources, cultural norms, and historical experience. The third, sociopolitical attitudes (external efficacy, internal efficacy, partisanship, interest in politics, trust in government), suggests that individuals with high levels of these attitudes are more likely to have a positive view of politics and government and thus have a greater probability of voting. Finally, the political environment also has a significant impact on voting (see Chapters 4–6). When elections are competitive and parties and candidates reach out to voters, citizens generally respond by showing up on Election Day and turnout is consequently higher. The key variables for the analysis in this chapter are those gauging a citizen's attitudes toward government and politics. In the previous section we found that during periods of divided government citizens had lower levels of external efficacy, political knowledge, interest in politics, and strength of partisan identification. If each of these variables is significantly related to the probability of voting while the other sets of predictors are controlled for, then we have a significant indirect relationship between the presence of divided government and the probability of voting.

Table 7.2 presents the probability of voting among registered citizens across the categories of external efficacy, political knowledge, interest in the current campaign, interest in public affairs, and strength of partisanship. The first section of Table 7.2 presents the predicted probability of voting across the three categories of external efficacy. As expected, individuals with a belief that the government is responsive to the demands of the electorate have a higher probability of stating they voted in the current election (4 points). Respondents who can correctly identify the majority party in the House of Representatives have a four point greater probability of stating they voted than those respondents who could not correctly identify the majority party. Interest in politics appears to have a fairly strong impact on the probability of voting. Respondents who stated that they were "very much interested" in the current campaign had a six percentage point higher probability of reporting a vote than respondents who stated that they were "not much interested." Respondents who stated that they followed governmental

TABLE 7.2   Probability of Voting Based on Political Attitudes

External Efficacy		
Low	Moderate	High
.91	.93	.95

Political Knowledge	
Incorrect	Correct
.88	.92

Interest in the Current Campaign		
Not Much Interested	Somewhat Interested	Very Interested
.89	.93	.95

Follow Public Affairs			
Hardly at All	Only Now and Then	Some of the Time	Most of the Time
.90	.92	.94	.95

Strength of Party Identification			
Independent	Leaner	Weak Partisan	Strong Partisan
.91	.92	.94	.95

Source: National Elections Study Cumulative File 1952–2002, Center for Political Studies, University of Michigan. The logistic coefficients from which these probabilities were calculated can be found in Appendix C.

and public affairs most of the time had a five percentage point greater likelihood of voting than respondents who stated that they followed governmental and public affairs "hardly at all." Finally, strong partisans have a four point greater probability of voting than pure independents.

These results are not surprising in that the relationships identified above are well established in the literature on individual-level electoral participation. Engaged and informed citizens who believe that elections can make a difference in policy outputs are more likely to take the time to vote than those who do not. Given that during divided government citizens have lower levels of these important attitudes, the pattern that Franklin and Hirzcy identified of lower turnout during periods of divided government is not surprising. What Franklin and Hirczy de Mino first identified and we have explored in this chapter is

TABLE 7.3   Difference in the Probability of Voting Between Unified/Divided Government Respondents Based on Political Attitudes

	Difference in the Probability of Voting
External efficacy	7%
Political knowledge	16%
Interest in the campaign	9%
Follow public affairs	4%
Strength of party Id	2%

Source: National Elections Study Cumulative File 1952–2002, Center for Political Studies, University of Michigan. The logistic coefficients from which these probabilities were calculated can be found in Appendix C.

a path analytic argument involving divided government and turnout. During periods of divided government many citizens come to believe that government is not responsive and find it difficult to assess governmental performance. Consequently many decide to abstain from voting. Based on this argument we should be able to identify the indirect effect of divided government on the probability of voting.

Table 7.3 presents the reduction in the likelihood of voting during periods of divided government because of its impact on our five key attitudinal variables.[12] As expected, due to reduced levels of external efficacy, respondents during periods of divided government were 7 percent less likely to state that they voted than respondents during periods of unified government. Due to reduced levels of knowledge divided government respondents had a 16 percent lower probability of reporting the vote than respondents during periods of unified government. The impact of divided government on citizens' interest in campaigns reduces turnout by 9 percent, while the effect working through interest in public affairs reduces the probability of voting by 4 percent. Decreased levels of partisanship during periods of divided government reduce the probability of voting by 2 percent.

The information presented in this chapter tends to confirm the argument that lessened responsiveness and blurred lines of accountability cause citizens to turn away from electoral politics during periods of divided government. Interestingly, divided government had its greatest impact on turnout by reducing levels of political knowledge. This pattern is not surprising. During periods of divided government, the ability of many citizens to "make sense" of the political world is greatly reduced. The blurred lines of accountability make it very difficult for citizens to know who is to receive credit or blame when control of the executive and legislative branches is split between the two parties. The muddied nature of politics during divided government increases the costs of information acquisition, to the extent that some are unable to correctly identify the majority party of the House of Representatives (Nicholson and Segura 1999). Divided government also reduces turnout by dampening citizens' interest in campaigns (9 percent). This most likely reflects an unclear informational environment during periods of divided government. A citizen who is having a difficult time assessing governmental performance may turn away from politics rather than pay the increased information costs. While the impact of divided government on turnout due to lowered levels of external efficacy results in large part from the lowered responsiveness of the government during these periods (lower levels of interest can also be interpreted as a symptom of dissatisfaction), it also reflects the weakened accountability of divided government. If citizens find it difficult to assess governmental performance, some citizens will likely come to believe that the government is not "doing its job" and elections therefore make little difference in policy formation.

While the second half of this chapter examined the impact of divided government on turnout, the overall chapter focus has been on the U.S. system of separation of powers. As Franklin and Hirczy de Mino note, given that the United States has the one true separation of powers system, we can't study the impact of the governing system on turnout across countries; but the potential for divided government in the U.S. system does provide the opportunity to study it across time. Divided government in a sense is a case study on the separation of powers. Divided government in the United States is an extreme form of separation of powers in that each branch is divided between two parties that may be bitterly opposed on important issues, with a predictable impact on attitudes and turnout. However, even during periods of unified government, our separation of powers system is still less responsive than the typical parliamentary system. Presidents do not always get what they ask of Congress, even one controlled by their party.[13] Accountability is also more difficult in our system than in a parliamentary system. There is little doubt in the average parliamentary system which party is responsible for government actions, since the government and majority party in parliament are one in the same. However, in our presidential–separation of powers system either side can pass the buck if the public becomes disenchanted and turnout declines. This system nonetheless has obvious strengths. For over two hundred years our separation of powers system has provided stability, checks on impulsive decisionmaking, and compromise. The by-product of this system, however, is that a portion of the electorate gets turned off by politics and therefore electoral turnout is lower.

Notes

1. The ability of the majority party in the British parliament to pass virtually all pieces of important legislation is strengthened by party discipline, or the tendency of party members to vote in line on important issues (Birch 1993).

2. Since 1960 the mean turnout rate in British parliamentary elections has been roughly 72 percent, which is much higher than the mean turnout in the United States but somewhat lower than the approximately 80 percent mean turnout rate for the other industrialized democracies considered in this book. Given that British parliamentary elections are based on single-member district, winner-take-all elections, the lower turnout is not surprising (see Chapter 4).

3. See the seminal report issued by the American Political Science Association Committee on Political Parties, "Toward a More Responsible Two-Party System," *APSR* 44, no. 3 (1950): pt. 2, supplement.

4. France is the only other industrialized democracy to have voluntary registration.

5. See Stimson (1999) for a thorough examination of the public mood.

6. For research supporting Mayhew's argument, see Fiorina (1996), Jones (1994), and Kreihbel (1996).

7. For the dialogue between Kelly and Mayhew, see Kelly (1993a,b) and Mayhew (1993).

8. In order to use the same questions for every year, the analyses used in this chapter are based on data from presidential election years from 1964 to 2000.

9. See Appendix B for a listing of the questions used in this analysis.

10. The predicted probabilities were calculated by using Clarify (Tomz, Wittenberg, and King 2003). The models from which the probabilities discussed in this chapter were estimated are in Appendix C. The models used in this chapter were estimated using only respondents registered to vote. The models for external efficacy, interest in the campaign, interest in public affairs, and strength of partisanship were estimated using ordered logistic analysis. The model for political knowledge was estimated using a simple logistic model.

11. To facilitate the calculation and interpretation of the probabilities, the external efficacy index was collapsed from eight categories (4–12) to three: low, medium, and high.

12. These indirect effects are calculated by multiplying the coefficient for divided government in the attitudinal models with the coefficient for a particular attitude in the turnout model. For instance, the 7 percent reduction in turnout for external efficacy is calculated as divided government coefficient (−.241) X external efficacy coefficient (.307) −.07. Because these are logistic coefficients, we take $e^{-.07}$, which gives us a log odds ratio of .93. This ratio is equivalent to a 7 percent reduction in the probability of voting due to the effects of divided government on citizens' level of external efficacy. See Appendix C for the actual models used in this chapter.

13. For example, in 1993 the newly elected President Clinton presented a Democratic-controlled Congress his plan for a national health care program. In the end the program was defeated in the face of stiff Republican opposition. In 2005 the Republican-controlled Congress passed a stem cell research bill in spite of President George W. Bush's opposition.

8

Conclusion

The Future of Electoral Reform in the United States

The discussion and analysis in the previous chapters established that the structure of elections and governance in the United States work to constrain turnout levels. Some have put forth arguments and data suggesting that low turnout does not matter. These arguments range from (1) low turnout is a symptom of a satisfied electorate (Berelson, Lazarfeld, and Mcphee 1954) to (2) the attitudes of nonvoters are similar to those of voters and thus the policy preferences of nonvoters are being represented by voters on Election Day; any increases in turnout would make little difference to the outcome (Gant and Lyons 1993; Highton and Wolfinger 2001; Wolfinger and Rosenstone 1980). This book operates from the position that while both arguments have merit and may in fact be true, elections are a matter of voice. If certain groups are not represented among voters (as is the case in American elections), then the government has less democratic legitimacy than one chosen by a broad range of groups in a society in which all groups participate in selecting leaders. This position understands low turnout as a problem that is worth the effort to remedy. In the remainder of this chapter we will examine ideas for increasing turnout in American elections.

Changing the Current System

Changing the core structure of American elections and governance would be very difficult and not necessarily desirable. For example, the separation of powers is the central feature of the constitutional structure and thus would require amending the Constitution to change, and there is no apparent support among the public for such a change. Additionally, while a change to a parliamentary system would most likely lead to a modest increase in turnout levels, it would come at the expense of a system that has provided relative stability for over two hundred years. Despite the reduced levels of responsiveness and accountability, the division of governmental power between the legislative and executive branches, which are both checked by an independent judiciary, has dampened impulsive decisionmaking since the founding. The costs of replacing our separation of powers system in the end would most likely outweigh the benefits.

In contrast, there is broad support for replacing the Electoral College. For example, a *Washington Post* poll taken on November 12, 2000, (during the aftermath of the 2000 presidential election controversy) showed that 63 percent of citizens polled favored replacing the Electoral College with the direct election of the president through a popular vote. Based on the analysis presented in this text, this change would most likely lead to a modest increase in national-level turnout. While there are arguments against eliminating the Electoral College, the costs of such a reform would be minimal. Consequently the elimination of the Electoral College would be a relatively low-cost way of increasing turnout in the United States. But the Electoral College is not likely to be abolished in the near future because it is part of the constitutional structure. An amendment to change the Constitution must be proposed by two-thirds (or 67 percent) of both Houses. In 1989 an amendment passed the House of Representatives supported by 83 percent of the members but was filibustered in the Senate (Dahl 2002), which would likely be the fate of another amendment to abolish the Electoral College. Because the allocation of electoral votes across the states is based on total congressional representation, small states are actually overrepresented in the Electoral College because of the equal representation in the Senate. Given this, constitutional amendments to abolish the Electoral College will have difficulty succeeding because (1) sixty-seven votes in the Senate will be next to impossible to achieve without the support of small states and (2) the amendment can be filibustered at any time.[1] As noted in Chapter 5, the Electoral College can easily be reformed at the state level, and the two most prominent potential reforms are proportional allocation of votes, or the district system now used in Maine and Nebraska. The proportional allocation of votes has the most promise for producing changes in turnout, as it would force the campaigns to fight for votes in each state to win electoral votes (see Chapter 5).

Franklin (2004) argues that one way to increase turnout in American elections is to increase competition in congressional elections. For example, eliminate single-member district winner-take-all House elections and move to some form of proportional representation system based on either national at-large elections or large multimember districts (Powell 1986; Jackman 1987; Jackman and Miller 1995). SMDs would be much simpler to eliminate than the Electoral College. Single-member districts are not part of the constitutional framework, and the system of elections could be easily replaced by repealing the 1967 law that mandates them. This change is not likely to be made, however. First, such a dramatic reform is not likely to garner support without some precipitating event convincing the public of a need for it (Kingdon 1984). Second, many citizens are likely to oppose the elimination of SMDs because they are happy with having a representative in Washington. In fact, the dyadic representation between a House member and his or her constituents is a strength of our SMD system. A possible solution would be to implement the German model. The Bundestag adds roughly three hundred at-large proportional seats to correct for the disproportionality of SMD. Given the higher levels of turnout associated with proportional representation, this reform would likely lead to modest increases in national turnout. Again, the dramatic nature of the reform would most likely stop action without some mobilizing event.

Any dramatic change to the core structures of the American electoral and governmental system will be difficult, if not impossible, to achieve. Therefore, reform efforts aimed at increasing turnout must focus on changes that can be made with relative ease, such as improving access to the ballot. Although registration reform will have limited success at increasing turnout (Franklin 2004; Highton 2004), other reforms may be achieved at the state level or by an act of Congress. The remainder of this concluding chapter will examine the limits and merits of reforms aimed at improving access to the voting booth.

Registration Laws

Since the passage of the Voting Rights Act of 1965, there has been a steady loosening of the requirement for voters to add their name to the list of registered citizens prior to casting a ballot. The two most prominent reforms, motor voter reforms and Election Day registration (EDR), sought to increase turnout by making the act of registration easier. Motor voter procedures were first implemented in Michigan in 1975, and were adopted by many states over the next fifteeen years. In 1993 Congress passed the NVRA, which mandated that all states (with the exception of those states with EDR and North Dakota, which has no registration requirement) provide for citizens to register to vote when they renew or acquire a driver's license, through the mail, or at certain public agencies. As discussed in Chapter 3, the impact of the reform since its implementation in 1995 has been limited. While the reform has enlarged the pool of registered voters and modestly improved the representativeness of the registered population, it has had no discernible impact on turnout levels. As the pool of eligible voters grows over time, turnout may increase (see Knack 1995; Hill 2003). While the NVRA cannot be considered a dramatic success, it has made registration more convenient for millions of Americans and has increased the pool of potential voters available for mobilization in competitive elections. Although the reform is unlikely to substantially increase turnout levels in the United States, it is a worthwhile part of a larger project to make voting more convenient.

Election Day registration (EDR) holds greater potential for increasing turnout on a national scale. Currently six states (see Chapter 3) have EDR in place, which apparently leads to greater turnout. Brians and Grofman (2001) estimate that the EDR procedures resulted in increases of seven percentage points in state-level turnout. However, EDR has done little to reverse the skew toward those of higher socioeconomic status in the electorate (Highton 1997; Brians and Grofman 2001). Although reforms such as this are usually implemented at the state level, as with the NVRA, EDR could easily be put in place at the national level through congressional action. While we can't predict the exact increase that would result from the implementation of EDR at the national level, it would likely lead to discernible increases in national-level turnout.[2]

Highton (2004) argues that we may have gone as far as we can with registration reform. While reforms such as the NVRA reduce the costs of registration, they do little to motivate newly registered people to actually vote; thus the future NVRA future impact should be limited. While nationwide EDR implementation would not boost turnout up to levels in other industrialized democracies, the work of Highton (1997) and Brians and Groffman (2001) suggests that EDR could increase turnout levels by between five and ten percentage points.

Early Voting

In 1991 the state of Texas began to allow citizens to cast ballots prior to Election Day (Stein and Garcia-Monet 1997). Since then, many states have implemented laws allowing citizens to cast ballots prior to Election Day. In the 2004 presidential election thirty-one states allowed citizens to cast ballots early or to request absentee ballots without providing a reason (Kiely and Drinkard 2004). Before the election some estimated that as many as 30 percent of ballots would be cast early (Hegland 2004). Early balloting may be done in two different ways.

First, in most states citizens can cast a ballot at the local election office a specified period of time prior to the election. In states with more liberal early voting procedures such as Texas, citizens can cast ballots in person at location such as "schools, fire stations, and other government buildings" (Stein and Garcia-Monet 1997, 657). Texas citizens can call the local elections office and request "curbside voting (www.sos.state. tx.us)." Second, early ballots can be sent through the mail. Traditionally, a citizen could receive an absentee ballot if he or she was physically unable to vote at the designated voting precinct due to illness or being out of town on Election Day. In recent years many states have loosened the requirements for receiving an absentee ballot, in effect creating early voting by mail. As with all state-level policies, early voting procedures vary by state; however, the logic in all states is the same. By allowing early voting, the state is making the act of voting more convenient by lengthening the time a citizen has to cast a ballot. The most ardent proponents of early voting argue that this should increase turnout because citizens who might otherwise abstain from voting due to hectic lives can now cast ballots (Stein and Garcia-Monet 1997).

The question is whether or not early voting increases turnout. Stein and Garcia-Monet (1997) found that early voting procedures led to modest increases in turnout at the county level in Texas elections, although whether the increases were due to partisan mobilization resulting from the early voting option is unclear. There is no evidence to suggest that early voting has any effect on the socioeconomic bias in the voting electorate (Neeley and Richardson 2001; Stein 1998). The voters who take advantage of early voting procedures are essentially the same voters who show up on Election Day. However, there are attitudinal differences between early voters and Election Day voters. Early voters were more likely to believe the outcome of the election is important and to take an interest in the campaign than Election Day voters (Neeley and Richardson 2001; Stein 1998) and more likely to be strong partisans (Stein 1998). Apparently the people voting early would have shown up on Election Day anyway but chose to "beat the crowds" and cast their ballots early (Neeley and Richardson 2001). The research discussed above all was based on one election in one state

(Stein et al. 1992, 1994 Texas Elections; Neeley and Richardson 2001, Tennessee General election) and thus should be viewed with caution when trying to extrapolate the impact of the reform into the future. The work does suggest that the impact of early voting will be to make the act of voting more convenient for engaged citizens and will have a slight impact on turnout at best.

Voting by Mail

Voting by mail was one of the early voting methods available to citizens in many states, generally in the form of absentee ballots. When a citizen is unable to cast a ballot at his precinct due to illness or absence, he can request an absentee ballot from the local election office that enables him to cast a ballot without reporting to the polling place. The work done on absentee voting suggests that these voters are older, have higher levels of income, and live in urban settings (Patterson and Caldeira 1985). When the parties actively target and mobilize potential absentee voters, the use of absentee ballots increases (Oliver 1996; Patterson and Caldeira 1985). Since the early 1980s states have liberalized their absentee voting laws, in effect creating the opportunity to vote by mail for all eligible citizens. In 1996 Oregon held the nation's first statewide election in which citizens could only cast ballots through the mail in a special election for the U.S. Senate and in 2000 began to conduct presidential elections completely through the mail (Karp and Banducci 2000). Mail-in voting is simple. Prior to an election, officials send out ballots to all registered voters, and they have a specified period of time to return the ballot. Given the simplicity and convenience of the process, mail-in voting should increase turnout, and some evidence suggests that voting by mail does lead to increases in turnout (Berinsky, Burns, and Traugott 2001; Karp and Banducci 2000; Southwell and Burchett 2000). However, the greatest impact appears to be in low-stimulus local elections. Additionally, as with the other reforms discussed here, the individuals casting ballots in these elections would have a high probability of voting anyway (older, white, educated, and high income) (Karp and Banducci 2000). Thus this reform does little to reduce the tendency of the American voting population to be skewed toward older, middle-class citizens.

Federal Holiday and Weekend Voting

In 1992 the House Post Office and Civil Service Committee approved a bill declaring Election Day an unpaid federal holiday. While employees would not be given the day off with pay as with other federal holidays, the logic behind "Democracy Day" was that creating a symbolic holiday would highlight the importance of Election Day and lead to a higher turnout (Michaelis 1992). In 1998 Martin Wattenberg argued in the *Atlantic Monthly* that one way to address the low turnout in American elections would be to move national elections from the current first Tuesday after the first Monday in November, which was established in 1872. Wattenberg suggests moving Election Day to the second Tuesday of November, which is Veteran's Day. By doing this, he argues, we could pay homage to those who served protecting our right to vote and celebrate democracy by going to the polls. Holding our national elections on Veteran's Day (or other holiday) would make the act of voting much less cumbersome since fewer voters would have to take time from a busy workday to cast a ballot. Because this reform has not been implemented, we can't really judge or accurately estimate its impact. However, research on other reforms aimed at making voting a more convenient act suggests that the overall impact would likely be to make voting more convenient for those already likely to vote.

The central argument for making Election Day a federal holiday is that currently individuals must take time to vote from a busy workday schedule. Another alternative would be to hold elections on a weekend. Currently six of the twenty nations considered in this text hold elections on weekends.[3] Franklin (1996, 2002, 2004) found that turnout in nations with weekend voting was indeed higher. However, he concludes that the implementation of weekend voting has little impact on turnout because an across time examination of weekend voting indicates that the implementation of weekend voting by a country results in no substantive change in turnout levels, nor does the change from weekend voting to weekday voting. It appears that the relationship between weekend voting and turnout is spurious, and the higher level of turnout in these countries is due to some other factor. Based on the research conducted on other forms of research, implementation of weekend voting would most likely be taken advantage of by those individuals most likely to vote. However, given that the reform has not been implemented in the United States, it is difficult to predict what impact the reform would have.

Internet Voting

In the 2004 presidential elections, the Pentagon, under its Federal Voting Assistance Program, planned to implement the secure registration and voting experiment (SERVE). Overseas citizens and military personnel from seven states would be able to register to vote and then actually cast ballots in the presidential primaries and general election. However, a report issued by four Internet security experts argued that the system was vulnerable to security breaches, and the $22 million program was canceled.[4] This rather ambitious program developed by the Defense Department fell victim to concerns about the security and thus integrity of the voting process.

Around the country, and indeed around the world, online voting is beginning to build momentum. Internet voting "is defined as the casting of a secure and secret electronic ballot that is transmitted to officials over the Internet" (Gibson 2001, 564; California Internet Voting Task Force 2000). Proponents of online voting argue that the increased convenience of balloting would increase participation in elections, particularly among young people who are comfortable using computers and navigating the Internet. Supporters also argue that online voting would increase administrative efficiency, for example, by reducing the number of paper ballots and the number of workers needed at polling places. Additionally, voting error would be reduced in that the software could notify the voter if a mistake had been made. The final count would also be made much easier. Counting errors should be reduced and the time it takes to tally the votes should also be reduced, given the electronic nature of the ballots (Gibson 2002). Critics respond that while online voting might be more convenient and efficient, it would be vulnerable to invasion of privacy of the voter's identification (the vote is supposed to be anonymous) and electronic intrusions into the tallying of the votes. The Internet is vulnerable to hackers and crimes such as identity theft, and thus elections held over the Internet would also vulnerable to attempts to "influence" the outcome of the final vote (see Rubin, Simons, and Wagner 2004).[5] Critics also argue that given the inequality in computer usage (younger and well-to-do citizens own computers and use the Internet, while older and poorer citizens do not), Internet voting will only exacerbate the inequality already present in electoral participation (Gibson 2002; Norris 2002). Opponents of online voting also argue that allowing citizens to vote at work, home, and other places will weaken the significance of voting. Voting is largely a public act and the "retreat" of citizens to vote in a private space weakens this important feature of electoral participation.

Few actual elections have included online voting. However, in 2000 the Arizona Democratic Party held its primary using Internet voting and thus we can examine this election to test the claims of supporters and critics of the reform. In terms of security there were no dramatic or clear cases of fraud; however, reports of personal identification numbers being acquired by landlords of tenants no longer living at a current address, an hourlong service interruption on the first day, and the refusal of the company running the election (Election.com) to open its procedures for scrutiny raised concerns among many that the security of the primary was less than adequate (Gibson 2001). Turnout in the Arizona primary may have been higher than in other primaries that year, although the media attention surrounding the use of the Internet may have led to increased participation (Gibson 2001; Solop 2001). In terms of equality in participation, it appears that while younger voters took advantage of the opportunity to vote online, middle-aged voters (36–55) voted online in the greatest numbers. As expected, more individuals with higher levels of income and education voted online than individuals from lower income and education groups. Men tended to vote online more than women and whites tended to vote online more than nonwhites (Gibson 2002; Solop 2001). All in all, the Arizona Democratic Party's experiment with Internet voting turned out as one would expect. There apparently were some security problems, and individuals most likely to have access to computers (and also those most likely to vote) were the ones taking advantage of the opportunity. Internet voting is a reform that most believe will become the norm in the future. At this point, however, the most prudent course of action is to continue to develop pilot programs and slowly phase in the use of the Internet in elections (California Internet Voting Task Force 2000).

All of the reforms discussed in this chapter have made limited impact on turnout and thus hold limited promise for substantial change in the future. However, all of the reforms to some extent make the process of voting easier and more convenient and thus reduce the costs of voting. Taken together, they should create a more convenient, accessible voting process in the United States. Turnout in the United States is greatly affected by institutional structures that are difficult to change, and thus reforming the voting process is the easiest and most practical approach, even given their limited impact. As the research on turnout and mobilization indicates, when the parties and candidates actively reach out to citizens, they respond by turning out to vote. Because of this, instituting all of the reforms discussed in this chapter would be a first step to increasing turnout in that they create a larger pool of potential voters for campaigns to mobilize and make it easier for individuals to cast a ballot once induced into voting by the campaign. With this in mind, then, what follows is a brief list of achievable recommendations to increase turnout in American elections. The recommendations are divided into two categories: (1) increasing access to the electoral process and (2) changing the nature of elections.

Increasing Access to
the Electoral Process

1. Election Day Registration. Given that turnout has been shown to increase following the implementation of Election Day registration at the state level, the implementation of this reform on a national scale would likely lead to noticeable increases in turnout. While the increase would not bring U.S. turnout levels up to those of other industrialized democracies, it would be a major step in the right direction.

2. Weekend Voting/Federal Holiday. There is no concrete evidence to suggest that weekend voting would lead to greater turnout. However, it would make voting easier for many citizens. Some have argued that making Election Day a holiday would also celebrate democracy, which could increase turnout due to heightened interest. Given the opposition to creating another federal holiday (or merging Election Day with Veterans' Day), weekend voting may be a practical alternative.

3. Early Voting/Mail-In Voting. Early voting would extend the length of time an individual citizen has to cast a ballot. This would allow the citizen to "schedule" the time of voting. Voting would become much more convenient in that a ballot would be sent to each citizen's house.

4. Internet Voting. At this point, the flaws associated with online voting far outweigh any potential benefits accrued from implementation of this reform. However, most analysts admit that Internet voting will become the norm in the future. Because of this, pilot projects and experimentation should continue until the flaws have been eliminated.

The recommendations suggested above have the immediate goal of making the act of voting more convenient.[6] While any reform elicits political opposition, these reforms can be implemented through congressional mandate or an incentive program from the federal government designed to induce states to implement them.

Changing the Nature of Elections

1. Proportional Allocation of Electoral Votes. The analysis presented in Chapter 5 indicates that the winner-take-all nature
   of the Electoral College forces campaigns to expend their resources in competitive states, and thus the nation is "unevenly
   mobilized." A move to proportional allocation of electoral
   votes, while not eliminating the tendency of campaigns to
   dedicate the bulk of their resources to the most competitive
   states, would create incentives for campaigns to devote resources to states where they have a chance of picking up votes
   even though they lose the popular vote in that state.
2. Public Campaign Financing. Franklin (2004) argues that a key
   problem with turnout in American elections is the lack of
   competition in congressional elections. Presidential turnout is
   shaped by congressional turnout in midterm elections, since
   the core voters (those who vote in both congressional elections
   and presidential elections) are determined in midterm congressional elections, and it is marginal voters who create the
   higher turnout in presidential elections. The core group of
   voters in congressional elections is small in large part due to
   the lack of competition in congressional elections. Increasing
   competition in congressional elections may be difficult. The
   increasing percentage of "safe" congressional seats witnessed
   in recent decades reflects the tendency of Americans to live in
   similar groups; for example, liberals tend to live in liberal
   neighborhoods, cities, and states, and conservatives behave
   similarly. Because of this red states have become more red, and
   blue states have become more blue (Abramowitz 2005).[7] Congressional districts have become less competitive also because
   incumbents outraise and outspend potential challengers (see
   Chapter 6). Because of this, public campaign financing in congressional elections is necessary to try to even the financial
   playing field between incumbents and challengers (Franklin
   2004). Although providing equal funds to candidates would

not overcome the natural advantages that incumbents have in congressional elections, it would bring all challengers up to the same level as incumbents in their ability to expend resources to gain votes. Given the positive impact of campaign spending on congressional challengers' vote totals, this reform is likely to increase the competition level of congressional elections. Politically this reform would be difficult to achieve and would face stiff opposition from Congress and the public. However, a phased approach of voluntary public funding (such as the system used at the presidential level and in many states) would help build public support for the reform.

All of the reforms discussed in this chapter will have a limited impact on turnout. The only way to substantially increase turnout to the levels found in other established democracies is to institute automatic registration, abolish the Electoral College, implement proportional representation in congressional (and state legislative) elections, and move to a parliamentary form of government without the separation of powers. Given that these reforms would be difficult to achieve, I have focused on reforms that can be achieved with relatively low political costs and seek to (1) make the act of voting easier (2) make the nature of our national elections more conducive to citizen participation. I began this book with a brief discussion of the 2004 presidential elections. By post-1960s American standards 2004 was a high-turnout election. Roughly 55 percent of the voting age population showed up to vote (60 percent of the voting eligible population) in response to what turned out to be a bitterly fought campaign to win the votes of a relatively divided country. The lesson to be learned from 2004 is that citizens will turn out to vote when they believe important issues are at stake (Polsby and Wildavsky 1991) *and* when the parties and candidates actively reach out to them. The political landscape of American politics will most likely remain in this relatively competitive state for the next several elections, and we should continue to witness higher levels of turnout. Matching the turnout levels achieved in other established democracies, however, will not be possible without institutional reform.

Notes

1. Filibusters can only be ended by invoking cloture which requires three-fifths of sixty votes.

2. The state legislature in Montana recently approved Election Day Registration and the reform is scheduled to be implemented in 2006. Election Day registration legislation was introduced in thirteen other states, although Montana is currently the only state to successfully pass the reform (Fitzgerald 2005).

3. This information was taken from the International Institute for Electoral Assistant website (www.idea.int). Germany's constitution mandates holding elections for the Bundestag on a Sunday or a holiday.

4. See "Security Analysis of the Secure Registration and Voting Experiment" by David Jefferson, Aviel D. Rubin, Barbara Simons, and David Wagner at www.servesecurityreport.org.

5. In 2001 the National Science Foundation released a report of a study conducted by a panel of experts stating that given security concerns Internet voting was not viable in the near future. The results of the study can be found at www.internetpolicy.org.

6. Highton and Wolfinger (2002) found that sending a sample ballot and information regarding the location of a citizen's polling place and increasing the length of voting hours lead to higher state-level turnout among registered citizens.

7. This argument is taken from an essay that Alan Abramowitz wrote for Larry Sabato's online website Crystal Ball, www.centerforpolitics.org/crystalball.

Appendix A

Country	Electoral System	Turnout, 1960–2000
Australia	Alternative Vote	83.74
Austria	List PR	84.79
Belgium	List PR	87.13
Canada	First past the post	66.74
Denmark	List PR	85.34
Finland	List PR	78.81
France	Two round (runoff)	64.86
Germany	Mixed/corrective	79.88
Iceland	List PR	89.06
Ireland	Single transferable vote	75.46
Israel	List PR	81.95
Italy	List PR[i]	92.15
Japan	Mixed/PR	67.75
Netherlands	List PR	83.00
New Zealand	First past the post	82.73
Norway	List PR	79.89
Sweden	List PR	84.64
Switzerland	List PR	40.60
United Kingdom	First past the post	72.50
United States	First past the post	54.65

Source: Institute for Democracy and Electoral Assistance. The data for the United States were aquired from the Federal Elections Commission

---

[i]In 1994 Italy changed its electoral rules to move from a list PR system to a mixed/corrective system that included single-member districts. In 1996 New Zealand changed its rules to move from a plurality system to a mixed/corrective system that included seats allocated through PR. Because the changes are relatively recent, both countries are classified as the systems they had in place prior to the changes. Italy is classified as a list PR system and New Zealand as a plurality system.

Appendix B

Questions Used from the
1948–2002 National Election Study Cumulative File

Interest in the Current Campaign: Some people don't pay much attention to political campaigns. How about you, would you say that you have been/were very much interested, somewhat interested, or not much interested in following the political campaigns (so far) this year?

Follow Public Affairs: Some people seem to follow what's going on in government and public affairs most of the time, whether there's an election going on or not. Others aren't that interested. Would you say you follow what's going on in government and public affairs most of the time, some of the time, only now and then, or hardly at all?

External Efficacy: Constructed from the following two questions. Please tell me you agree or disagree with these statements:

1. I don't think public officials care much what people like me think. Do you agree, neither agree nor disagree, or disagree with this statement?
2. People like me don't have any say about what the government does. Do you agree, neither agree nor disagree, or disagree with this statement?

Internal Efficacy: Please tell me you agree or disagree with this statement:

Sometimes politics and government seem so complicated that a person like me can't really understand what's going on.

Political Knowledge: Do you happen to know which party had the most members in the House of Representatives in Washington before the elections this month? (Prior to the election)

Strength of Partisanship: Measured as folded scale built from the traditional seven point party identification scale. The seven-point scale is based on the following questions:

1. Generally speaking, do you usually think of yourself as a Republican, a Democrat, an Independent, or what?
2. (IF REPUBLICAN OR DEMOCRAT) Would you call yourself a strong (REP/DEM) or a not very strong (REP/DEM)?
3. (IF INDEPENDENT, OTHER, or NO PREFERENCE) Do you think of yourself as closer to the Republican or Democratic party?

Questions Used from the
1999 European Union Election Study

Strength of Party Attachment: Do you feel yourself to be very close to this party, fairly close, or merely a sympathiser?

Interest in Politics: To what extent would you say you are interested in politics? Are you very interested, somewhat interested, a little interested, or not at all interested?

Internal Efficacy: I will read you a few statements that are often made. Could you say whether you strongly agree, agree, disagree, or strongly disagree with the following statements?

1. Sometimes politics is so complicated that someone like me just cannot understand what is going on.

External Efficacy: I will read you a few statements that are often made. Could you say whether you strongly agree, agree, disagree or strongly disagree with the following statements?

1. Parties and politicians in [name of your country] are more concerned with fighting each other than with furthering the common interest.

Appendix C

Ordered Logit/Logit Estimates of Interest in Campaigns, Interest in Public Affairs. Strength of Party Identification, Political Knowledge, and External Efficacy, 1964–2000

	Interest in Campaign	Interest in Public Affairs	Strength of Party ID	Political Knowledge	External Efficacy
Education	.147**	.160**	−.067**	.253**	.146**
	(.011)	(.010)	(.010)	(.014)	(.011)
Age	.018**	.023	.017**	.014**	−.006**
	(.001)	(.001)	(.001)	(.001)	(.001)
Gender	−.122**	−.519**	.237**	−.663**	.095**
	(.035)	(.034)	(.034)	(.046)	(.036)
South	−.164**	−.110**	−.002	.025	.093*
	(.041)	(.039)	(.039)	(.052)	(.040)
Black	.228**	−.003	.824**	−.679**	−.278**
	(.064)	(.061)	(.063)	(.074)	(.063)
Latino	−.181	−.316**	.114	−.331	−.229*
	(.101)	(.096)	(.098)	(.121)	(.101)
Other	.036	−.155	−.181	0.125	−.297**
	(.102)	(.099)	(.098)	(.124)	(.101)
Internal efficacy	.349**	.464**	.018	−.166	.255**
	(.033)	(.032)	(.031)	(.064)	(.034)
Outparty	.090*	.134**	.521**	−.100*	−.009
	(.036)	(.034)	(.034)	(.047)	(.036)
Ideology	.040*	.054**	.058	.066**	.006
	(.016)	(.015)	(.015)	(.021)	(.016)
Financial situation last year	−.211**	−.269**	−.081**	.028	−.134**
	(.024)	(.023)	(.022)	(.031)	(.023)
External efficacy	.142**	.139**	.042**	.048**	-----
	(.008*)	(.008)	(.008)	(.011)	
Strength of party identification	.276**	.086**	-----	.138**	.101**
	(.019)	(.018)		(.025)	(.019)
Interest in campaign	-----	-----	.391**	.333**	.277**
			(.027)	(.036)	(.028)
Interest in public affairs	-----	-----	−.014	.418**	.223**
			(.021)	(.027)	(.022)
Know majority party	.377**	.336**	.193**	-----	.084**
	(.033)	(.031)	(.031)		(.033)
Trust in government	−.006**	−.005**	.006**	−.005**	.032**
	(.001)	(.001)	(.001)	(.001)	(.001)
Divided government	−.161**	−.098*	−.100*	−.445**	−.228**
	(.043)	(.041)	(.041)	(.056)	(.044)
Psuedo R-square	.07	.08	.04	.14	.11
N	12,357	12,377	12,330	11,677	12,352

*=p<.05
**p<.01
Standard errors are in the parentheses

Logistic Estimates of the Probability of Voting, 1964–2000

	Unstandardized Coefficient	Standard Error
Education	.216**	.047
Age	.088**	.010
Age squared	−.001**	.0001
Gender	.158*	.069
South	.586*	.074
Black	−.362**	.104
Latino	−.199	.165
Other	−.740**	.155
Financial situation last year	−.061	.047
Trust in Government	−.001	.001
Internal efficacy	−.001	.064
Ideology	.063	.034
Strength of party identification	.204**	.035
Interest in campaign	.484**	.053
Interest in public affairs	.253**	.040
Know majority party	.404**	.072
External efficacy	.307**	.047
Divided government	.012	.091
Presidential margin	−.001	.003
Statewide election	−.024	.668
Purge registration rolls	.071	.068
Registration laws	−.033	.070
N	11,698	
Psuedo R-square	.14	
Log likelihood	−3154.8006	

*=p<.05
**p<.01
Standard errors are in the parentheses

Acknowledgments

I view this book as the culmination of a project I began in graduate school to understand voter turnout. Although countless people helped me carry out this work, the following were crucial. Larry Dodd was a valuable mentor and friend during and following graduate school who offered support and encouragement as I worked on this project. Michael Martinez served as a mentor, coauthor, and friend and provided sound methodological and professional advice. Steve Craig, Ken Wald, Margaret Conway, and Wayne Francis all played key roles in my professional development. Kyle Saunders provided helpful comments in the early phases of this project, and Seth Mckee helped me develop many of these ideas as we worked on our paper exploring the impact of the Electoral College on turnout. Daron Shaw and Gary Jacobson graciously provided data that made this project doable, and colleagues at Bridgewater State College and Valdosta State University offered advice and feedback over the past four years. I am forever indebted to my mother for giving me the attitude that I can do whatever I want to do, to my stepfather for passing on the discipline to complete whatever I start, and to my father for giving me the part of him that didn't view the world through the same lenses as everyone else. Finally, I would like to extend my love and thanks to my wife and daughter, who are the center and purpose of my life.

References

Abramowitz, Alan I. 2005. "Don't Blame Redistricting for Uncompetitive Elections." *Crytstal Ball*. http://www.centerforpolitics.org/crystalball.

Abramson, Paul R., and John H. Aldich. 1982. "The Decline of Electoral Participation in America." *American Political Science Review* 76, no. 3: 502–521.

Aldrich, John H. 1993. "Rational Choice and Turnout." *American Journal of Political Science* 37, no. 1: 246–278.

Almond, Gabriel A., and Sidney Verba. 1963. *The Civic Culture: Political Attitudes and Democracy in Five Nations*. Princeton: Princeton University Press.

Ansolabehere, S., and S. Iyengar. 1995. *Going Negative: How Political Advertisements Shrink and Polarize the Electorate*. New York: Free Press.

Ansolabehere, S., S. Iyengar, and A. Simon. 1999. "Replicating Experiments Using Aggregate and Survey Data: The Case of Negative Advertising and Turnout." *American Political Science Review* 93, no. 4: 901–909.

Ansolabehere, S., S. Iyengar, A. Simon, and N. Valentino. 1994. "Does Attack Advertising Demobilize the Electorate?" *American Political Science Review* 88, no. 4: 829–838.

Banks, Arthur S., ed. 1997. *Political Handbook of the World*. New York: McGraw-Hill.

Bartels, L. M. 1985. "Resource Allocation in a Presidential Campaign." *Journal of Politics* 47, no. 4: 928–936.

Bennett, Stephen Earl, and Linda L.M. Bennett. 1993. "Out of Sight, Out of Mind: Americans' Knowledge of Party Control of the

House of Representatives, 1960–1984." *Political Research Quarterly* 46, no. 1: 67–80.

Berelson, Bernard R., Paul F. Lazarsfeld, and William N. McPhee. 1954. *Voting*. Chicago: University of Chicago.

Berinsky Adam J. , Nancy Burns, and Michael W. Traugott. 2001. "Who Votes by Mail? A Dynamic Model of the Individual-Level Consequences of Voting-by-Mail System," *Public Opinion Quarterly*, 65: 178–197.

Bibby, John F. 2003. *Politics, Parties, and Elections in America*. 5th ed. Belmont: Thomson.

Birch, Anthony, H. 1993. *The British System of Government*. Ninth Edition. London: Routledge.

Blais, Andre. 2000. *To Vote or Not to Vote: The Merits and Limits of Rational Choice Theory*. Pittsburgh: University of Pittsburgh Press.

Blais, Andre, and R. K. Carty. 1991. "The Psychological Impact of Electoral Laws: Measuring Duverger's Elusive Factor." *British Journal of Political Science* 21: 79–93.

Blais, Andre, and Louis Massicotte. 1996. "Electoral Systems." In *Comparing Democracies: Elections and Voting in Global Perspective*, edited by Lawrence LeDuc, Richard G. Niemi, and Pippa Norris, 49–81. Thousand Oaks, Calif.: Sage.

_____. 2000. *To Vote or Not to Vote: The Merits and Limits of Rational Choice Theory*. Pittsburgh: University of Pittsburgh Press.

Blais, Andre, Louis Massicotte, and R. K. Carty. 1991. "The Psychological Impact of Electoral Laws: Measuring Duverger's Elusive Factor." *British Journal of Political Science* 21: 79–93.

Brams, S. J., and M. D. Davis. 1974. "The 3/2's Rule in Presidential Campaigning." *American Political Science Review* 68, no. 1: 113–134.

Brians, Craig Leonard, and Bernard Grofman. 2001. "Election Day Registration's Effect on U.S. Voter Turnout." *Social Science Quarterly* 82, no. 1: 170–183.

Brody, Richard. 1978. "The Puzzle of Political Participation in America." In *The New American Political System,* edited by A. King,

287–324. Washington, D.C.: American Enterprise Institute for Public Policy Research.

Brown, Robert D., Robert A. Jackson, and Gerald C. Wright. 1999. "Registration, Turnout, and State Party Systems." *Political Research Quarterly* 52, no. 2: 463–479.

Bullock, C. S., III, R. K. Gaddie, and A. Ferrington. 2002. "System Structure, Campaign Stimuli, and Voter Falloff." *Journal of Politics* 64, no. 4: 1210–1224.

Caldiera, Gregory A., Samuel C. Patterson, and Gregory A. Markko. 1985. "The Mobilization of Voters in Congressional Elections." *Journal of Politics* 47, no. 4: 490–506.

California Internet Voting Task Force. 2000. "A Report on the Feasibility of Internet Voting." http://www.ss.ca.gov/executive/ivote/final_report.pdf.

Campbell, Angus. 1960. "Surge and Decline: A Study of Electoral Change." *Public Opinion Quarterly* 24: 397–418.

Campbell, Angus, Philip E. Converse, Warren E. Miller, and Donald E. Stokes. 1960. *The American Voter*. New York: Wiley.

Clinton, J. D., and J. S. Lapinski. 2004. "'Targeted' Advertising and Voter Turnout: An Experimental Study of the 2000 Presidential Election." *Journal of Politics*, 66, no. 1: 69–96.

Colantoni, C. S., T. J. Levesque, and P. C. Ordeshook. 1975. "Campaign Resource Allocation Under the Electoral College." *American Political Science Review* 69, no. 1: 141–154.

Coleman, John J. 1999. "Unified Government, Divided Government, and Party Responsiveness." *American Political Science Review* 93: 821–835.

Converse, Philip. 1972. "Change in the American Electorate." In *The Human Meaning of Social Change*. Edited by Angus Campbell and Philip Converse, 263-337. New York: Sage Foundation.

Conway, Margaret M. 1981. "Political Participation in Congressional Midterm Electionism." *American Politics Quarterly* 9: 221–244.

_____. 2000. *Political Participation in the United States*. 3rd ed. Washington, D.C.: Congressional Quarterly Press.

Cox, G. W., and M. C. Munger. 1989. "Closeness, Expenditures, and Turnout in the 1982 U.S. House Elections." *American Political Science Review* 83, no. 1: 217–230.

Craig, Stephen C. 1985a. "The Decline of Partisanship in the United States: A Reexamination of the Neutrality Hypothesis." *Political Behavior* 7: 57–59.

_____. 1985b. "Partisanship, Independence, and No Preference: Another Look at the Measurement of Party Identification." *American Journal of Political Science*. 29, no. 2: 274–290.

_____. 1987. "Neutrality, Negativity, or Both? A Reply to Wattenberg." *Political Behavior* 9: 126–138.

_____. 1993. *The Malevolent Leaders: Popular Discontent in America*. Boulder: Westview.

Craig, Stephen C., Richard G. Niemi, and Glenn E. Silver. 1990. "Political Efficacy and Trust: A Report on the NES Pilot Study Items." *Political Behavior* 12: 289–314.

Crawford, Susan E.S., and Elinor Ostrom. 1995. "A Grammar of Institutions." *American Political Science Review* 89, no. 3: 582–600.

Crewe, Ivor. 1981. "Electoral Participation." In *Democracy at the Polls*, edited by David Butler, Howard Penniman, and Austin Ranney. Washington, D.C.: American Enterprise Institute.

Dahl, Robert, A. 2002. *How Democratic Is the American Constitution?* New Haven: Yale University Press.

Delli Carpini, Michael X., and Scott Keeter. 1996. *What Americans Know About Politics and Why It Matters*. New Haven: Yale University Press.

_____. 1985. "The Cycles of Legislative Change." In *Political Science: The Science of Politics*, edited by Herbert Weisberg, 82–103. New York: Agathon.

Dodd, Lawrence C. 1977. "Congress and the Quest for Power." In *Congress Reconsidered*. First edition. Edited by Lawrence C. Dodd and Bruce I. Oppenheimer. New York: Praeger.

_____. 1985. "The Cycles of Legislative Change." In *Political Science: The Science of Politics*. Edited by Herbert Weisberg. New York: Agathon Press.

Dodd, Lawrence C., and Terry Sullivan. 1981. "Majority Party Leadership and Partisan Vote Gathering: The House Democratic Whip System." In *Understanding Congressional Leadership*, edited by Frank H. Mackaman, 227–260. Washington, D.C.: Congressional Quarterly.

Downs, Anthony. 1957. *An Economic Theory of Democracy*. New York: Harper & Row.

Duverger, Maurice. 1954. *Political Parties*. London: Methuen.

Edwards, George C., III, Andrew Barrett, and Jeffrey Peake. 1997. "The Legislative Impact of Divided Government." *American Journal of Political Science* 41: 545–563.

Erikson, Robert S. 1981. "Why Do People Vote? Because They Are Registered." *American Politics Quarterly* 9, no. 3: 259–276.

Erikson, Robert S., and Thomas R. Palfrey. 1998. "Campaign Spending and Incumbency: An Alternative Simultaneous Equations Approach." *Journal of Politics* 60: 355–373.

Fenster, Mark J. 1994. "The Impact of Allowing Day of Registration Voting on Turnout in U.S. Elections from 1960 to 1992." *American Politics Quarterly* 22, no. 1: 74–87.

Finkel, S., and J. Geer. 1998. "A Spot Check: Casting Doubt on the Demobilizing Effect of Attack Advertising." *American Journal of Political Science* 42, no. 2: 573–595.

Fiorina, Morris P. 1989. *Congress: Keystone of the Washington Establishment*. New Haven: Yale Univeristy Press.

———. 1996. *Divided Government*. 2nd ed. Boston: Allyn & Bacon.

Fitzgerald, Mary. 2005. "The Triggering Effects of Election Day Registration on Partisan Mobilization Activities in the U.S. Elections." Paper presented at the annual meeting of the American Political Science Association, Washington, D.C., September 1–4, 2005.

Franklin, Mark N. 1996. "Electoral Participation." In *Comparing Democracies: Elections and Voting in Global Perspective*, edited by Lawrence LeDuc, Richard G. Niemi, and Pippa Norris, 216–235. Thousand Oaks, Calif.: Sage.

_____. 2004. *Voter Turnout and the Dynamics of Electoral Competition in Established Democracies Since 1945*. Cambridge: Cambridge University Press.

Franklin, Mark N., and Wolfgang Hirczy de Mino. 1998. "Separated Powers, Divided Government, and Turnout in U.S. Presidential Elections." *American Journal of Political Science* 42, no. 1: 316–326.

Franklin, Mark N., and Diana Evans. 2000. "The Low Voter Turnout Problem." In *The U.S. House of Representatives: Reform or Rebuild?* Edited by Joseph F. Zimerman and Wilma Rule, 97–113. Westport, Conn.: Praeger.

Freedman, P., and K. M. Goldstein. 1999. "Measuring Media Exposure and the Effects of Negative Campaign Ads." *American Journal of Political Science* 43, no. 3: 1189–1208.

Fridkin Kahn, Kim, and Patrick J. Kenney. 1999. "Do Negative Campaigns Mobilize or Suppress Turnout? Clarifying the Relationship between Negativity and Participation." *American Political Science Review* 93, no. 4: 877–889.

Gaddie, Ronald Keith, and Charles S. Bullock III. 2000. *Elections to Open Seats in the U.S. House: Where the Action Is*. Lanham, Md.: Rowman & Littlefield.

Gant, Michael M., and William Lyons. 1993. "Democratic Theory, Nonvoting, and Public Policy: The 1972–1988 Presidential Elections." *American Politics Quarterly* 21, no. 2: 185–204.

Gerber, A. S., and D. P. Green. 2000. "The Effects of Canvassing, Telephone Calls, and Direct Mail on Voter Turnout: A Field Experiment." *American Political Science Review* 94, no. 3: 653–663.

_____. 2001. "Do Phone Calls Increase Voter Turnout? a Field Experiment." *Public Opinion Quarterly* 65, no. 1: 75–85.

Gerber, Elizabeth R., Rebecca B. Morton, and Thomas A. Reitz. 1998. "Minority Representation in Multimember Districts." *American Political Science Review* 92, no. 1: 127–144.

Gibson, Rachel. 2001. "Elections Online: Assessing Internet Voting in Light of the Arizona Democratic Primary." *Political Science Quarterly* 116, no. 4: 561–583.

Gilliam, Frank D. 1985. "Influences on Voter Turnout for U.S. House Elections in Non-Presidential Years." *Legislative Studies Quarterly* 10: 339–351.

Goldstein, K. M., and P. Freedman. 2002. "Campaign Advertising and Voter Turnout: New Evidence for a Stimulation Effect." *Journal of Politics* 64, no. 3: 721–740.

Green, Donald P., and Jonathon S. Krasno. 1988. "Salvation for the Spendthrift Incumbent." *American Journal of Political Science* 32: 844–907.

———. 1990. "Rebuttal to Jacobson's 'New Evidence for Old Arguments.'" *American Journal of Political Science* 34: 363–372.

Green, D. P., and I. Shapiro. 1994. *Pathologies of Rational Choice Theory: A Critique of Applications in Political Science.* New Haven: Yale University Press.

Hegland, Corrine. 2004. "When 'Tuesday' Is 40 Days Long." *National Journal* 36, no. 41: 3042–3047.

Highton, Benjamin. 1997. "Easy Registration and Voter Turnout." *Journal of Politics* 59, no. 2: 565–575.

———. 2004. "Voter Registration and Turnout in the United States." *Perspectives on Politics* 2, no. 3: 507–515.

Highton, Benjamin, and Megan Mullin. 2002. "How Postregistration Laws Affect the Turnout Among Citizens Registered to Vote." *State Politics and Policy Quarterly* 5, no. 1: 1–23.

Highton, Benjamin, and Raymond E. Wolfinger. 1998. "Estimating the Effects of the National Voter Registration Act of 1993." *Political Behavior* 20, no. 2: 79–104.

———. 2001. "The Political Implications of Higher Turnout." *British Journal of Political Science* 31, no. 1: 202–210.

———. 2001. "The First Seven Years of the Political Life Cycle." *American Journal of Political Science* 45, no. 1: 202–209.

Hill, David. 2003. "A Two-Step Approach to Assessing Composition Effects of the National Voter Registration Act." *Electoral Studies* 22: 703–720.

Hill, David, and Seth Mckee. 2005. "The Electoral College, Mobilization, Turnout in the 2000 Presidential Election." *American Politics Research* 33, no. 5: 700–725.

Hill, Kim Quaile, and Jan E. Leighley. 1993. "Party Ideology, Organization, and Competitiveness as Mobilizing Forces in Gubernatorial Elections." *American Journal of Political Science* 37, no. 4: 1158–1178.

_____. 1996. "Political Parties and Class Mobilization in Contemporary United States Elections." *American Journal of Political Science*, 40, no. 3: 787–804.

_____. 1999. "Racial Diversity, Voter Turnout, and Mobilizing Institutions in the United States." *American Politics Quarterly*, 27, no. 3: 275–295.

IDEA. International Institute for Democracy and Electoral Assistance. www.idea.int.

"Into the Final Straight." 2004. *Economist* 373, no. 8399: 31–33.

Jackman, R. W. 1987. "Political Institutions and Voter Turnout in the Industrial Democracies." *American Political Science Review* 81, no. 2: 405–423.

_____. 1993. "Rationality and Political Participation." *American Journal of Political Science* 37, no. 1: 279–290.

Jackman, R. W., and Ross A. Miller. 1995. "Voter Turnout in the Industrial Democracies During the 1980s." *Comparative Political Studies* 27, no. 4: 467–492.

Jackson, Robert A. 1996. "A Reassessment of Voter Mobilization." *Political Research Quarterly* 49, no. 2: 331–349.

_____. 1996. "The Mobilization of Congressional Electorates." *Legislative Studies Quarterly* 21, no. 3: 425–445.

_____. 1997. "The Mobilization of U.S. State Electorates in the 1988 and 1990 Elections." *Journal of Politics* 59, no. 2: 520–537.

_____. 2000. "Differential Influences on Participation in Midterm Versus Presidential Elections." *Social Science Journal* 37, no. 3: 385–402.

Jacobson, Gary C. 1978. "The Effects of Campaign Spending in Congressional Elections." *American Political Science Review* 72: 469–491.

_____. 1980. *Money in Congressional Elections*. New Haven: Yale University Press.

_____. 1985. "Money and Votes Reconsidered: Congressional Elections, 1972–1982." *Public Choice* 47: 7–62.

_____. 1990. "The Effects of Campaign Spending in House Elections: New Evidence for Old Arguments." *American Journal of Political Science* 34: 334–362.

_____. 2004. *The Politics of Congressional Elections*. New York: Longman.

James, S. C., and B. L. Lawson. 1999. "The Political Economy of Voting Rights Enforcement in America's Gilded Age: Electoral College Competition, Partisan Commitment, and the Federal Election Law." *American Political Science Review* 93, no. 1: 115–131.

Jefferson, David, Aviel D. Rubin, Barbara Simmons, and David Wagner. 2004. "A Security Analysis of the Secure Electronic Registration and Voting Experiment (Serve)." www. servesecurityreport.org.

Jones, Charles O. 1994. *The Presidency in a Separated System*. Washington, D.C.: Brookings Institution.

Jones, J. 1998. "Does Bringing Out the Candidate Bring Out the Votes? The Effect of Nominee Campaigning in Presidential Elections." *American Politics Quarterly* 26, no. 4: 395–419.

Kahn, K. F., and P. J. Kenney. 1999. "Do Negative Campaigns Mobilize or Suppress Turnout? Clarifying the Relationship Between Negativity and Participation." *American Political Science Review* 93, no. 4: 877–890.

Karp, Jeffrey A., and Susan A. Banducci. 2000. "Going Postal: How All-Mail Elections Influence Turnout." *Political Behavior* 23, no. 3: 223–239.

Kelly, Sean Q. 1993a. "Divided We Govern: A Reassessment." *Polity* 25: 475–484.

_____. 1993b. "Response: Let's Stick with the Larger Question." *Polity* 25: 489–490.

Kiely, Kathy, and Jim Drinkard. 2004. "Early Voting Growing in Size and Importance." *USA Today,* September 28, 13.

Kingdon, John W. 1984. *Agendas, Alternatives, and Public Policies.* Boston: Little, Brown.

Kleppner, Paul. 1982. *Who Voted? The Dynamics of Electoral Turnout, 1870–1980.* New York: Praeger.

Knack, Stephen. 1995. "Does 'Motor Voter' Work? Evidence from State Level Data." *Journal of Politics* 57, no. 3: 796–811.

_____. 1999. "Drivers Wanted: Motor Voter and the Election of 1996." *PS: Political Science and Politics,* June 2, 237–243.

Krasno, Jonathan S., and Donald P. Green. 1988. "Preempting Quality Challengers in House Elections." *Journal of Politics* 50: 920–936.

Kreihbel, Keith. 1996. "Institutional and Partisan Sources of Gridlock: A Theory of Divided and Unified Government." *Journal of Theoretical Politics* 8: 7–40.

Lane, Robert. 1959. *Political Life: Why and How People Get Involved in Politics.* New York: Free Press.

Leighley, Jan E., and Jonathon Nagler. 1992. "Socioeconomic Bias in Turnout, 1964–1988: The Voters Remain the Same." *American Political Science Review* 86, no. 3: 725–736.

Lijphart, Arend. 1984. *Democracies: Patterns of Majoritarian and Consensus Government in Twenty-One Countries.* New Haven: Yale University Press.

Lutz, Donald, Philip Abbott, Barbara Allen, and Russell Hansen. 2002. "The Electoral College in Historical and Philosophical Perspective." In *Choosing a President,* edited by Paul D. Schumaker and Burdett A. Loomis. New York: Chatham House.

Madison, James. 1961. The Federalist # 56. In *The Federalist.* New York: The Modern Library.

_____. 1961. *The Federalist* # 57. In The Federalist. New York: The Modern Library.

March, James G., and Johan P. Olsen. 1989. *Rediscovering Institutions: The Organizational Basis of Politics.* New York: Free Press.

Martinez, Michael D., and David Hill. 1999. "Did Motor Voter Work?" *American Politics Quarterly* 27, no. 3: 296–315.

Mayer, William G., Emmett H. Buell Jr., James E. Campbell, and Mark Joslyn. 2002. "The Electoral College and Campaign Strategy." In *Choosing a President,* edited by Paul D. Schumaker and Burdett A. Loomis. New York: Chatham House.

Mayhew, David R. 1974. "Congressional Elections: The Case of the Vanishing Marginals." *Polity* 6: 259–317.

_____. 1991. *Divided We Govern: Party Control, Lawmaking, and Investigations, 1946–1990.* New Haven: Yale University Press.

_____. 1993. "Let's Stick with the Longer List." *Polity* 25: 485–488.

McDonald, M. P. 2002. *U.S. State Turnout Rates for Eligible Voters, 1980–2000.* Inter-University Consortium for Political and Social Research, no. 1248.

McDonald, M. P., and Samuel L. Popkin. 2001. "The Myth of the Vanishing Voter." *American Political Science Review* 95, no. 4: 963–974.

Michaelis, L. 1992. "House Panel Would Declare Unpaid Federal Holiday." *Congressional Quarterly Weekly Report* 50, no. 11: 618.

Mitchell, Glenn E., and Christopher Wlezien. 1995. "The Impact of Legal Constraints on Voter Registration, Turnout, and the Composition of the American Electorate." *Political Behavior* 17, no. 2: 179–202.

Moss, Jordan. 1993. "Motor Voter: From Movement to Legislation." *Social Policy* 24, no. 2: 21–33.

Neeley, Grant W., and Lilliard E. Richardson Jr. 2001. "Who Is Voting Early: An Individual Level Examination." *Social Science Journal* 38: 381–392.

Nicholson, Stephen P., and Gary M. Segura. 1999. "Midterm Elections and Divided Government: An Information Driven Theory of Electoral Volatility." *Political Research Quarterly* 52, no. 3: 609–629.

Niemi, Richard G., Stephen C. Craig, and Franco Mattei. 1991. "Measuring Internal Political Efficacy in the 1988 National Election Study." *American Political Science Review* 85: 1407–1413.

Norris, Pippa. 2002. "E-Voting as the Magic Bullet? The Impact of Internet Voting on Turnout in European Parliamentary Elections." Paper prepared for the workshop on e-voting and the European Parliamentary Elections, Villa La Fonte, EUI, May 10–11, 2002.

Oliver, J. Eric. 1996. "The Effects of Eligibility Restrictions and Party Activity on Absentee Voting and Overall Turnout." *American Journal of Political Science* 40: 498–513.

Patterson, Samuel C., and Gregory A. Caldiera. 1985. "Mailing In the Vote: Correlates and Consequences of Absentee Voting." *American Journal of Political Science* 29, no. 4: 766–788.

Patterson, T. E. 2002. *The Vanishing Voter: Public Involvement in an Age of Uncertainty*. New York: Knopf.

Piven, Frances Fox, and Richard A. Cloward. 1983. "Toward a Class-Based Realignment of American Politics." *Social Policy* 13, no. 3: 3–14.

———. 1996. "Northern Bourbons: A Preliminary Report on the National Voter Registration *Act*." *PS: Political Science and Politics* 29, no. 1: 39–42.

———. 2000. *Why Americans Don't Vote*. New York: Pantheon.

Polsby, Nelson W., and Aaron Wildavsky. 1991. *Presidential Elections: Contemporary Strategies of American Electoral Politics*. New York: Free Press.

Powell, G. B., Jr. 1986. "American Voter Turnout in Comparative Perspective." *American Journal of Political Science* 80, no. 1: 17–43.

Powell, G. Bingham, Jr. 1986. "American Voter Turnout in Comparative Perspective." *American Journal of Political Science* 80, no. 1: 17–43.

———. 2000. *Elections as Instrument of Democracy: Majoritarian and Proportional Visions*. New Haven: Yale University Press.

Public Law 103–31, 1993, 107 Stat. 77–89.

Radcliff, Benjamin. 1992. "The Welfare State, Turnout, and the Economy: A Comparative Analysis." *American Political Science Review* 86, no. 2: 444–454.

Rae, Douglas W. 1967. *The Political Consequences of Electoral Laws.* New Haven: Yale University Press.

Rhine, Stacy. 1995. "Registration Reform and Turnout Change in the American States." *American Politics Quarterly* 23, no. 4: 409–427.

Riker, William H. 1986. "Duverger's Law Revisited." In *Electoral Laws and Their Political Consequences*, edited by Bernard Grofman and Arend Lijphart. New York: Agathon.

Riker, W. H., and P. C. Ordeshook. 1968. "A Theory of the Calculus of Voting." *American Political Science Review* 62, no. 1: 25–42.

Rosenstone, Steven J. 1982. "Economic Adversity and Voter Turnout." *American Journal of Political Science.* 26, no. 1: 25–46.

Rosenstone, Steven J., and Raymond E. Wolfinger. 1978. "The Effect of Registration Laws on Turnout." *American Political Science Review* 72, no. 1: 22–45.

———. 1982. "Economic Diversity and Voter Turnout." *American Journal of Political Science* 26, no. 1: 25–46.

Rosenstone, Steven J., and J. M. Hansen. 1993. *Mobilization, Participation, and Democracy in America.* New York: Macmillan.

———. 2001. "Solving the Puzzle of Participation in Electoral Politics." In *Controversies in Voting Behavior*, edited by R. G. Niemi and H. F. Weisberg. 4th ed. Washington, D.C.: CQ Press.

Rusk, Jerrold. 1970. "The Effect of the Australian Ballot Reform on Split Ticket Voting: 1876–1908." *American Political Science Review*: 1220–1238.

Schick, Rupert, and Wolfgang Zeh. 1999. *The Germany Bundestag: Functions and Procedures.* NDV, Rheinbreitbach.

Serra, George. 1994. "What's in It for Me? The Impact of Congressional Casework on Incumbent Evaluation." *American Politics Quarterly* 22: 403–420.

———. 1995. "Citizen-Initiated Contact and Satisfaction with Bureaucracy: A Multivariate Analysis." *Journal of Public Administration Research and Theory* 5: 175–188.

Serra, George, and Albert D. Cover. 1995. "The Electoral Impact of Casework." *Electoral Studies* 14: 171–177.

Shaw, D. R. 1999. "The Methods Behind the Madness: Presidential Electoral College Strategies, 1988–1996." *Journal of Politics* 61, no. 4: 893–913.

———. 2004. "The Truth About Electoral College Strategies." Manuscript.

Smith, Terrence. 1977. *Abstracts Information Bank Abstracts*, 10. New York: New York Times Company.

Solop, Frederic I. 2001. "Digital Democracy Comes of Age: Internet Voting and the 2000 Arizona Democratic Primary." *PS: Political Science and Politics* 34, no. 2: 289–293.

Solop, Frederic I., and Nancy A. Wonders. 1995. "The Politics of Inclusion: Private Voting Rights Under the Clinton Administration." *Social Justice* 22, no. 2: 67–87.

Southwell, Priscilla, and Justin Burchett. 2000. "Does Changing the Rules Change the Players? The Effect of All-Mail Elections on the Composition of the Electorate." *Social Science Quarterly* 81, no. 3: 837–845.

Squire, Peverill, Raymond E. Wolfinger, and David P. Glass. 1987. "Residential Mobility and Voter Turnout." *American Political Science Review* 81, no. 1: 45–65.

Stein, Robert M. 1998. "Early Voting." *Public Opinion Quarterly*. 57–69.

Stein, Robert M., and Patricia Garcia-Monet. 1997. "Vote Early But Not Often." *Social Science Quarterly* 78, no. 3: 657–671.

Stein, Robert M., Paul Johnson, Daron Shaw, and Robert Weissberg. 2002. "Citizen Participation and Electoral College Reform." In *Choosing a President,* edited by Paul D. Schumaker and Burdett A. Loomis. New York: Chatham House.

Stimson, James A. 1999. *Public Opinion in America: Moods, Cycles, and Swings.* Boulder: Westview.

Syrett, Harold C., and Jacob E. Cooke (eds). 1961. *The Papers of Alexander Hamilton.* New York. Columbia University Press.

Taagepera, Rein, and Matthew Soberg Shugart. 1989. *Seats and Votes: The Effects and Determinants of Electoral Systems*. New Haven: Yale University Press.

Timpone, Richard J. 1998. "Structure, Behavior, and Voter Turnout in the United States." *American Political Science Review* 92, no. 1: 145–158.

Tomz, Michael, Jason Wittenberg, and Gary King. 2003. Clarify: Software for Interpreting and Presenting Statistical Results. Version 2.1. http://gking.harvard.edu.

Verba, Sidney, Kay Lehman Schlozman, and Henry Brady. 1995. *Voice and Equality: Civic Volunteerism in American Politics*. Cambridge: Harvard University Press.

Washington Post–ABC News Post-Election Poll, November 12, 2000. http://www.washingtonpost.com/wp-srv/politics/polls/vault/data111300.htm.

Wattenberg, Martin P. 1996. *The Decline of American Political Parties, 1952–1994*. Cambridge: Harvard University Press.

———. 1998. "Should Election Day Be a Holiday?" *New Republic*, October, 42–46.

Wattenberg, M. P., and C. L. Brians. 1999. "Negative Campaign Advertising: Demobilizer or Mobilizer?" *American Political Science Review* 93, no. 4: 891–899.

Wielhouwer, P. W. 2000. "Releasing the Fetters: Parties and the Mobilization of the African-American Electorate." *Journal of Politics* 62, no. 1: 206–222.

Wielhouwer, P. W., and B. Lockerbie. 1994. "Party Contacting and Political Participation, 1952–1990." *American Journal of Political Science* 38, no. 1: 211–219.

Wielhouwer, P. W., and S. J. Rosenstone. 1980. *Who Votes?* New Haven: Yale University Press.

Wolfinger, Raymond E., and Johnathon Hoffman. 2001. "Registering and Voting with Motor Voter." *PS: Political Science and Politics* 34, no. 1: 85–92.

Wolfinger, Raymond E., and Steven. J. Rosenstone. 1980. *Who Votes?* New Haven: Yale University Press.

Index

absentee ballots. *See* mail-in
  voting (absentee ballots)
accountability, 29, 115–132, 134
Adams, John Quincy, 91n. 10
advertising
  and mobilization efforts,
    19–20, 81–82
  negative, 20, 31, 81
  spending on, distribution of,
    75–79
  television, 31n. 11, 75–76,
    81–82
AFDC (Aid to Families with
  Dependent Children), 35, 39
African Americans, 3, 34. *See
  also* racial minorities
age, statistics based on, 44–48
Aldrich, John H., 23
alternative vote (AV) elections,
  60
Arizona, 142–143
Arkansas, 34
Atlantic Monthly, 140
Austin, Richard, 35
Australia, 9n. 5, 18, 69n. 2
AV (alternative vote) system, 60

base states, 75, 76
battleground (swing) states,
  75–79, 83–89
Belgium, 9n. 5, 69n. 2
Bennett, Stephen Earl, 122, 124
bicameral systems, 28
Blais, Andre, 21, 23, 31n. 13
Brady, Henry, 11–12
Brians, C. L., 53, 54, 137
Brody, Richard, 3
Brown, Robert D., 42
Bullock, C. S., 99, 100–101
Bundestag, 135, 147n. 3. *See also*
  Germany
Burnham, Walter D., 34–35
Bush, George Herbert Walker,
  38–39, 113n. 11
Bush, George W., 1, 84, 90n. 9

calculus, of voting, 21–24, 102
California, 35–36
Campaign
  financing, 145–146
  spending, 97–112
Campbell, Angus, 94
Canada, 18

Carter, Jimmy, 36
casework, 96–97
Census Bureau, 112n. 1
Center for Political Research, 121
Civic Culture (Almond and Verba), 16–17
civic volunteerism model, 11–12, 19–20
Civil Service Committee, 140
Civil War, 90n. 7
Cleveland, Grover, 91n. 10
Clinton, Bill, 39–40, 132n. 14
Cloward, Richard A., 34, 37
coalition governments, 66
Coleman, John J., 120
communism, 27
compulsory voting, 26, 40–41, 69n. 2
Congress, 24–25, 29. *See also* House of Representatives
  and campaign spending, 97–112
  and district-level competitiveness, 93–114
  and midterm elections, 94–95
  and mobilization efforts, 19–20
  open seats in, 99–101
  and plurality rules, 62–63
  and registration laws, 33–34, 36
  and the separation of powers, 29, 116, 117, 119
  the Voting Rights Act, 35

Congress: Keystone of the Washington Establishment (Fiorina), 96–97
conservatives, 27
Constitution, 33–35, 63
  amendments to, 5–6, 35, 90n. 4, 134–135
  and the Electoral College, 71–73, 87, 88, 90n. 4
  and registration laws, 33–34
  and the separation of powers, 134
  and SMD elections, 62–63
Constitutional Convention, 72
constituency service, 96–97
Cox, G. W., 80, 102, 106
culture, types of, 16–17
curbside voting, 138

Defense Department, 141
"Democracy Day," 140
Democratic Party. *See also* partisanship
  and registration laws, 38, 39
  and unified governments, 120
  and winner-take-all elections, 75
demographics, 25, 43–48, 80
Denmark, 9n. 5, 30n. 4
discrimination, 34, 35
disproportionality, in vote translation, 28
District of Columbia, 71

districts, 67–69, 89, 93–114. *See also* SMD (single-member district) elections
divided government, periods of, 29, 115–132
Downs, Anthony, 21
driver's license bureaus, 35, 37. *See also* NVRA (National Voter Registration Act)
Dukakis, Michael, 113n. 11
Durverger, Maurice, 65–66

early voting, 137–139, 144
EC (Electoral College), 24–25, 68–93, 124, 145
  and campaign strategy, 73–79
  and increased citizen involvement, 85–87
  and plurality rules, 62
  and winner-take-all elections, 71–92
economic downturns, 13
Economic Theory of Democracy, An (Downs), 21
EDR (Election Day registration), 42–54, 136–138, 144
  Brians and Grofman on, 53, 54
  impact of, 52–54
  and marginal groups, 53–54
  and registration laws, 36, 38–39, 42–45, 48–54
education
  and LSDV estimates, 83
  as a predictor of individual-level turnout, 12, 13

registration statistics based on, 44–48
Edwards, George C., 120
efficacy
  external, 15–16, 18, 122–124, 127, 130, 132n. 13
  internal, 14–15, 16
Election Day registration. *See* EDR (Election Day registration)
elections. See *specific types*
Electoral College. *See* EC (Electoral College)
electoral laws, defined, 26
Erikson, Robert S., 41, 99
ethnic minorities, 44–48, 107. *See also* minorities
European Election Study, 18, 30n. 7, 152–153
executive responsiveness, 115–132, 134
external efficacy, 15–16, 18, 122–124, 127, 130, 132n. 13

"faithless electors," 90n. 5
FEC (Federal Election Commission), 2, 41, 43, 68, 72
federal holiday voting, 140–141, 144
Federalist Papers, 62
Fiorina, Morris, 96–97
food stamp offices, 35, 39
France, 1, 26, 41, 68

Franklin, Mark N., 94, 126,
128–130, 140–141
on declining turnout, 3–4
on divided government,
121–122, 124
on the frequency of elections,
32n. 19
on increasing turnout, 135
on the lack of competition, in
congressional elections, 145
on midterm elections, 94, 112
on the separation of powers, 5,
6, 28–29, 117, 118, 122, 124
fraud, voting, 34, 36, 39

Gaddie, Ronald Keith, 99,
100–101
Garcia-Monet, Patricia, 138
Georgia, 63, 71
Gerber, A. S., 19, 20
Germany, 1, 69n. 1, 135, 147n. 3
Glass, David P., 46
Gore, Albert, 84, 90n. 9
GOTV (get out the vote efforts),
19. *See also* mobilization
Great Britain, 1, 116, 131n. 1,
131n. 2
Greece, 18
Green, D. P., 19, 20, 99, 113n. 7
GRPs (gross rating points), 76,
78, 82, 84, 91n. 13, 92n. 20
gubernatorial races, 19–20, 78
and LSDV estimates, 83
and OLS estimates, 107

Hamilton, Alexander, 62–63
Hansen, J. M., 20, 82
Harrison, Benjamin, 91n. 10
Hayes, Rutherford B., 91n. 10
Highton, Benjamin, 48, 53–54,
137, 147n. 6
Hispanic Americans, 45–48
Hoffman, Johnathon, 49
holiday voting, 140–141, 144
House of Representatives, 16, 71,
73, 77–78. *See also* Congress
and district-level
competitiveness, 93–114
and the Electoral College, 87,
89
as an example of a political
institution, 24–25
House Post Office, 140
and midterm elections, 94–95
open seats in, 99–101
and plurality rules, 62
and registration laws, 38
and the separation of powers,
117
and SMD elections, 62–63, 68
Human Development Report
(United Nations), 30n. 3
Human Serve (nonprofit
organization), 37

Idaho, 52
immigrants, 34. *See also* ethnic
minorities

income levels, 12–13, 83, 107. *See also* socioeconomic status model
incumbents, 95–100, 102–104
  and campaign spending levels, 110–112
  and the path turnout model, 102–104
independent voters, 126
Indiana, 34
institutions
  examples of, 24–25
  role of, 24–30
internal efficacy, 14–15, 16
International Institute for Democracy and Electoral Assistance, 2, 41
Internet voting, 141, 143–144
Ireland, 30n. 4
Israel, 18, 68
Italy, 1, 69n. 2

Jackman, R. W., 6, 18–19, 26–28
Jackson, Robert A., 42, 95, 102–107
Jacobson, Gary C., 98, 112n. 1
Japan, 18
Jefferson, Thomas, 90n. 4
Jim Crow laws, 34
Johnson, Paul, 89

Kelly, Sean Q., 119–120
Kerry, John, 1
Kleppner, Paul, 33–35
Knack, Stephen, 48, 51–52

knowledge, political, 15–16, 122
Krasno, Jonathon S., 99, 113n. 7

Latino Americans, 46, 107
Lehman Schlozman, Kay, 11–12
Lijphart, Arend, 65
list system, 60
LSDV (least squares dummy variable), 78, 82–83, 92n. 16
Luxemburg, 18

Madison, James, 62
mail-in
  registration, 36, 38, 42–43, 45
  voting (absentee ballots), 139–140, 144
Maine, 36, 62, 89, 135
majoritarian systems, 59–61, 67
manual labor jobs, 27
March, James G., 25
marginal states, 75
Martinez, Michael D., 49
Maryland, 63
Mayhew, David R., 119
McDonald, Michael, 8n. 1, 9n. 6
McKee, Seth, 78–79, 82, 84
Michigan, 35, 37, 38
midterm elections, 94–95, 105–108, 112
military personnel, 141
Miller, Ross A., 19, 26
Minnesota, 36
Mino, Hirzcy de, 118, 121, 126, 128–130

minorities, 34, 44–48. *See also*
    African Americans; ethnic
    minorities
Mitchell, Glenn E., 41–42
mobilization, 19–20, 26–27, 136,
    139–140
  and Internet voting, 143
  and registration laws, 37–38
  and SMD systems, 67
  and winner-take-all elections,
    71–92
Montana, 147n. 2
motor voter programs, 35, 45,
    136. *See also* NVRA
    (National Voter Registration
    Act)
multivariate regression, 77
Munger, M. C., 80, 102, 106

National Association of
    Secretaries of State, 38
National Election Study (NES),
    30n. 7, 121–122, 125,
    151–152
National League of Cities, 38
National Science Foundation,
    147n. 5
Nebraska, 62, 89, 135
negative advertising, 20, 31, 81.
    See also advertising
Netherlands, 68
New Hampshire, 52
New York State, 38
New Zealand, 18
Nicholson, Stephen P., 122, 124

North Dakota, 36–37, 39, 53–54,
    136
Norway, 9n. 5, 30n. 4
NVRA (National Voter
    Registration Act), 36–55,
    136–137. *See also* motor
    voter programs
  described, 36–40
  impact of, 55
  and social groups, statistics
    based on, 45, 47

Ohio, 36, 38
OLS (ordinary least squares),
    104–107
Olson, Johan P., 25
open seat elections, 99–101,
    104–110
Oregon, 139
overseas citizens, 141

paradox, of voting, 22
parliamentary governments, 79,
    134, 146
  as examples of political
    institutions, 24–25
  and the separation of powers,
    116–117, 121, 129, 131
parochial culture, 16
participant culture, 17
partisanship, 14–15, 17, 123, 126
path turnout model, 102–104
Patterson, Thomas, 86–87
Pennsylvania, 35–36
Pentagon, 141

Piven, Frances Fox, 34, 37
Planned Parenthood, 37
plurality systems, 59–64, 66–67,
   69
political advertising
   and mobilization efforts,
      19–20, 81–82
   negative, 20, 31, 81
   spending on, distribution of,
      75–79
   television, 31n. 11, 75–76,
      81–82
political efficacy, 14–15, 16, 17
poll taxes, 34
pork barrel politics, 97
Portugal, 18
Powell, G. Bingham Jr., 6, 18,
   26–27, 40, 55, 67, 69
PR (proportional
   representation) systems,
   59–61, 64–66, 68
presidential elections. *See also*
   EC (Electoral College)
   and absentee ballots, 139
   and campaign strategy, 73–79
   candidate visits by
      battleground status during,
      76–77
   and early voting, 137
   estimates of resource
      allocation in, 77–78
   and Internet voting, 141
   and midterm elections, 94–95
   and mobilization efforts,
      19–20

and plurality systems, 67
and rational choice, 22–23
and registration laws, 40–41
and the separation of powers,
   116
year 2000, 72–73, 79, 86, 134,
   140
year 2004, 1, 137, 141
pro-business voters, 27
Progressivism, 34
property requirements, 34
proportional systems, 28
psychological engagement,
   14–19

racial minorities, 44–48, 83, 107.
   See also African Americans
Radcliffe, Benjamin, 13
rational choice, 21–24
Reagan, Ronald, 38
Reconstruction, 34
recruitment, 19–20. *See also*
   mobilization
registration. *See also* registration
   laws
   history of, 33–40
   as a key component of
      turnout, 25, 26
   and rational choice, 22
registration laws, 7–8, 136–139.
   See also registration
   defined, 25
   impact of, 33–58
   and social groups, 43–48

Republican Party. *See also*
   partisanship
   and presidential elections, 1
   and registration laws, 38–39
   and unified governments, 120
   and winner-take-all elections,
      75
residency requirements, 34, 35,
   44–48
responsiveness, executive,
   115–132, 134
Rosenstone, Steven J., 13, 20, 40,
   52, 82
RPM (responsible party model),
   117
runoff elections, 60

Scandinavian nations, 1
"second order" elections, 94. *See*
   also midterm elections
Segura, Gary M., 122, 124
separation of powers, 5–7,
      115–132, 134, 146
   and Congress, 116, 117, 119
   Franklin on, 5, 6, 28–29, 117,
      118, 122, 124
September 11th terrorist attack,
   119
SERVE (secure registration and
   voting experiment), 141
SES groups, 47, 54, 49
Shaw, Daron, 80, 82, 89, 91n. 12
SMD (single-member district)
   elections, 7, 59–64, 67–69,
   135

and disproportionality, 28
eliminating, 135
history of, 62–63
and mobilization, 26–27
and plurality systems, 59–60,
   62, 69
and the role of institutions, 24
and turnout comparisons, 64
socialism, 27
Social Policy (journal), 37
socioeconomic status model,
   11–14, 44–48
South Carolina, 72, 90n. 7
Squire, Peverill, 46
states
   base, 75, 76
   battleground (swing), 75–79,
      83–89
Stein, Robert M., 89, 138
STV (single-transferable vote)
   system, 61
subject culture, 16
Supreme Court, 35
"surge and decline" theory, 94
Sweden, 9n. 5
swing states. *See* battleground
   (swing) states
Switzerland, 9n. 5, 30n. 4, 32n.
   19, 70n. 4

TANF (Temporary Assistance for
   Needy Families), 37
tax requirements, 34

television advertising, 31n. 11,
75–76, 81–82. *See also*
advertising
terrorism, 119
Texas, 34, 38, 137–138
Tilden, Samuel, 91n. 10
Twelfth Amendment, 90n. 4
Twenty-Fourth Amendment, 35
Twenty-Sixth Amendment, 5–6,
35
two-party systems, 65–66

underclass, 7, 37
unemployment offices, 39
unicameral systems, 28
unions, 37
United Nations, 30n. 3, 30n. 4
Universal Voter Registration Act,
36

Vanishing Voter, The (Patterson),
86–87
VAP (turnout rate for all
individuals of voting age), 1,
8n. 1
VEP (turnout rate for all
citizens), 1, 8n. 1
Verba, Sidney, 11–12, 16–17, 19
Veteran's Day, 140
voter eligibility requirements.
See registration laws
Voting Rights Act, 35–36, 136

Washington Post, The, 134
Wattenberg, Martin, 140
weekend voting, 140–141, 144
Weissberg, Robert, 89
welfare state, 13
white-collar occupations, 13, 27
winner-takes-all elections, 7–8,
71–114
and battleground states,
75–79, 83–89
and campaign spending,
97–112
and disproportionality, 28
and the Electoral College,
71–92
eliminating, 135
and mobilization, 27, 71–92
and presidential elections,
71–92
and the role of institutions, 24
and U.S. House elections,
93–114
Wisconsin, 35–36
Wlezien, Christopher, 41–42
Wolfinger, Raymond E., 40, 46,
48–49, 52, 147n. 6
women, provision of suffrage to,
34
working class, 34
World War II, 3, 5, 29, 96
Wright, Gerald C., 42
Wyoming, 52